Grow old along with me
the best is yet to be

Other anthologies from Sandra Haldeman Martz

When I Am an Old Woman I Shall Wear Purple

If I Had a Hammer:
Women's Work in Poetry, Fiction, and Photographs

The Tie That Binds: A Collection of Writings about
Fathers & Daughters / Mothers & Sons

If I Had My Life to Live Over I Would Pick More Daisies

I Am Becoming the Woman I've Wanted

Threads of Experience
With Fabric-and-Thread Images by Deidre Scherer

Grow old along with me the best is yet to be

Edited by
Sandra Haldeman Martz

Papier-Mache Press
Watsonville, CA

Large Print Edition 1996

05 04 03 02 01 00 99 98 97 96   10 9 8 7 6 5 4 3 2 1

ISBN: 0-918949-96-3 Softcover

Editorial Support by Shirley Coe
Copyediting by Candace Atkins
Cover art "Counterpoint" © 1995, fabric and thread by Deidre Scherer
Cover design by Cynthia Heier
Interior design by Leslie Austin
Text composition by Deborah Karas
Proofreading by Erin Lebacqz
Editor photograph by Thomas Burke
Manufactured by Malloy Lithographing, Inc.

**This Large Print Book carries the
Seal of Approval of N.A.V.H.**

Library of Congress Cataloging-in-Publication Data

Grow old along with me: the best is yet to be / edited by Sandra Haldeman Martz.
    p. cm.
    ISBN 0-918949-96-3 (softcover: alk. paper)
    1. Large type books. 2. Aging—Literary collections. 3. Aging, Writings of the, American.
4. American literature—20th century.
I. Martz, Sandra.
[PS509.A37G76   1996]
810.8'354—dc20   95-52419
                                                             CIP

For Dan

Contents

Editor's Preface

My professional interest in the subject of aging began in the early 1980s when as a new editor and publisher I compiled *When I Am an Old Woman I Shall Wear Purple,* an anthology of poetry, prose, and photographs exploring women and aging. Both the book and the process of creating it changed my life in ways I could not have envisioned: defining my life's work, redefining my attitudes about growing older, and connecting Papier-Mache Press with readers and writers around the world.

While editing *Grow Old Along with Me—The Best Is Yet to Be,* I reflected on how this anthology differs from its predecessor. The answer is found, I feel, in both the social changes that have occurred in the last ten years and in the changed perspectives of the writers. Much of the material in *When I Am an Old Woman I Shall Wear Purple* was written in the early eighties. About half of the writers in the collection were in their mid-forties or younger, women my age. They painted tender word pictures of mothers and grandmothers and older women friends. They, and I, viewed aging earnestly, poignantly, tenderly—and with a certain distance.

Today my generation is firmly entrenched in middle age, marching stalwartly ahead of the baby boomers. Two-thirds of the women writers whose work was selected for

Grow Old Along with Me are over fifty; one-third are over sixty. This is our story now: our age spots, our menopause, our arthritic bones.

Our expectations about growing older have shifted dramatically in the last decade, influenced by the prospect of longer life spans, increased awareness of health and fitness, more positive media images of older women, and the changed perceptions of women's roles in a world that grew out of the social movements of the sixties and seventies. We expect to be taken more seriously—by politicians, by the medical community, by our religious leaders, by our families. But we also demand the freedom to take life less seriously—to be unconventional, to flaunt our grey hair and wrinkles, to be age proud. It's an exciting time to be an older woman.

Compiling *Grow Old Along with Me* also provided the opportunity to look at another perspective on aging: how men feel about growing older. Over the last several years an increasing number of men have attended anthology readings around the country. Their level of interest in the issues discussed and their enthusiasm about participating in this type of emotionally evocative exploration of aging prompted me to broaden the scope to include both men and women.

For most of my editorial life, my work has focused on women writers and women's issues. I wasn't sure what kind of material to expect from male writers. Any assumptions I had, however, were challenged by my commitment to keep an open ear, an open heart.

In the end the differences between what men and

women had to say about aging were minor. The men in the stories and poems seemed a little more likely to define themselves through their work, to be more reflective about the mark they felt they had (or had not) made on the world, or to be more anxious about retirement and what they would do with their lives afterward. But these issues also surfaced for some of the women. The women in the stories and poems generally seemed better prepared for their old age, more excited about new beginnings as family structures shifted. Yet there were also men on the brink of new adventures and experiencing new personal insights. Particularly satisfying were the writers who spoke from the other side's point of view—men writing about women and women writing about men—the result, perhaps, of writers who are really caring listeners.

Common threads ran throughout the material: the need to be loved, the importance of family connections, an acceptance of the aging process. There were observable differences when the writings were grouped by age of the characters in the stories. Self-assessment, both physical and psychological, was most likely to emerge in the stories and poems depicting people in their fifties and early sixties. Those in their late sixties and seventies often focused on letting go, retirement, loss of life partners. The very old were especially eloquent when celebrating life's simplicity.

It is hard to find the right words to describe the photographs. Beautiful. Courageous. Tender. Vigorous. Joyful. They stand alone as visual poems. They complement and illuminate the text. The work would not be the same without them.

As with the previous anthologies, only a very small percentage of the total submissions could appear in this collection (eighty poems, stories, and photographs drawn from more than 7,000 pieces submitted from across the U.S. and Canada). However, all of the material helped to inform and shape the finished work. Reflecting the hopes, fears, joys, and sorrows of a community of writers, I feel certain that the authors also speak for the larger community of women and men, old and young, who are transforming the terrain of old age. Their words leave me challenged and eager to greet the future. I invite you, dear reader, to "Grow old along with me—the best is yet to be."

—*Sandra Haldeman Martz*

Grow old along with me!
The best is yet to be,
The last of life, for which the first was made:
Our times are in His hand
Who saith 'A whole I planned,
Youth shows but half; trust God: see all, nor be afraid!'

—Robert Browning
"Rabbi Ben Ezra"

photo by Marianne Gontarz

Manon Reassures Her Lover
Martha Elizabeth

When I cannot sleep, I stroke you,
and like a napping cat that purrs
and stretches when touched, you linger
with pleasure on the edge of waking,
curling far into slumber. You know
that I am watching, you are safe.
Your skin is soft, smells fresh.

I love how your face is sculpted,
the drapes and furrows, how your cheek
laps over your forearm as you sleep.
I love how your skin moves under my hand,
the way it sags on the muscle and bone,
as the skin of a ripe peach
slips loose almost without the knife.

I have no hunger for young flesh,
unripe, firm but tasteless by comparison.
You are still at the very peak
of ripeness, sweet, with the tang
that quenches thirst. I would like
to take a gentle bite from your shoulder,
golden in the faint light from the window.

Letting Go
Allison Joseph

I wear no bra, abandon
hooks and closures,
let my body drift
into its own idea
of adulthood, my skin
less firm, scars
and stretch marks
showing me how far
I've come, telling me
I'm no longer young,
that this body will
record all I do on
its ledger: every callus,
every spidery vein,
every bit of pleasure.
Now, I can touch knees
no longer smooth
or enticing, feel arms
that have held too many
boxes of books,
shrug shoulders
that stoop a little now,

closer to the ground,
to life. I don't bother
to guess where this body's
going, to predict its
passions or motions,
preferring its surprises—
arms reaching farther
than I thought they could,
legs walking me into towns
I don't know. Wiser,
saner, my body goes
where it wants, knowledge
of sinew and cell all
it needs to know,
all it wants to tell.

Deeper, Wider, Finer
Peter Cooley

Each dawn for the man a new face
swims up in his shaving mirror.
The eyes stare back, in charge of everything:
the jawbone, the nose, each year more like his father,
both twisted a little to the left, cubistic,
rearranged by a seventh grade football accident.
It is all here: the new day glazed
in stubble he will scrape like an engraver
burning the plate with fine lines of his razor
while he creates himself—as while he slept,
after sex the night before or during his rush
into the woman or late today at his desk—
so too the sculptor will be at work on him,
pulling the lines at the sides of his eyes wider,
deepening the crevices on both sides of his nose,
crossing the brow with cross-stitching of its trade,
preparing the corpse handsomely, masterfully,
for his rightful position among contemporaries.

photo by Teresa Tamura

In the Autumn
William Borden

In the autumn of the year, in the autumn of his life, he waded into the dry, brown leaves as if he were walking into the sea. He marched knee-deep, the leaves spraying and flying—a dusty splashing, like hopes crumbling. He inhaled the dust of his life.

The afternoon was cloudy, and the air was chill. The park was empty. As he climbed the hill, leaves crawled up his socks and pecked at his legs. Leaves flew up to grab at his jacket and trousers, and he remembered walking through the field beside his house when he was eight and the tall grass exploding with grasshoppers. They landed on his pants, on his shirt, clinging to him in desperation, like refugees from a war zone. He ran, flailing at them.

His grandfather would hold a grasshopper between his thumb and forefinger and touch his other forefinger to the grasshopper's mouth. A drop of brown liquid would appear on his fingertip. "Tobacco juice," his grandfather would say. The boy believed him.

His grandfather knew magic. It was a magical spell, a verse from the Bible, and it stopped bleeding. He remembered the time his grandfather was sitting under the tree in the front yard, smoking his pipe, and he, the boy, ran out to tell him that his brother had cut his hand.

Grandpa nodded. He kept on sitting and puffing on the

scarred, blackened pipe as if nothing in the world had changed. It was a secret spell, repeated silently in the mind. Within minutes the bleeding stopped, and the boy went out to tell his grandfather, so his grandfather could stop saying the spell and go back to whatever it was he went back to in his mind.

When the boy was a teenager and his grandfather was in the nursing home, nothing seemed to be going on in his grandfather's head. He visited his grandfather regularly at first, and the old man seemed glad to see him. His grandfather's thin, weak hand reached up from the bed to grasp the boy's hand. The old man smiled, and his eyes teared a little.

The nursing home smelled like all nursing homes. He didn't know what the odor came from—urine, medicine, age, sadness, the embrace of death—maybe all combined. Autumn has a smell. It's the scent of dead leaves crackling underfoot, crumbling, collapsing into dust, as corpses finally do.

After a few months, his grandfather's eyes, filmed by a membrane of moisture, seemed not to recognize him. When the boy went to the bed where his grandfather was supposed to be and looked at the frail figure there between the railings of the bed—all the beds had railings, like cribs—it was not the man who had pinched tobacco juice from grasshoppers' mouths. Yet the boy recognized something.

When his grandfather died, it was ascribed to old age. How could old age be a killer? As easily as, say, middle age—a disease he could imagine never recovering from. He could picture himself keeling over, at eighty, from the effects of middle age. Old age attacked the joints and spilled brown spots over the skin; it sunk cheeks, dimmed eyes, dropped teeth. But middle age—middle age attacked the mind, the soul, the way one thought about things. It was insidious, as sneaky as water rising silently in the basement when no one's looking.

None of his middle-aged friends had died yet. They and he were more subject to breaks and strains—those little deaths of autumn. Four winters ago he had slipped on the ice and broken his leg. His wife had tripped on the stairs and broken her arm; she had a plastic elbow now. There were among his friends broken ribs, migraines, bad teeth, and almost universal lower back pain.

There were books that told of people dying and then returning—visions of light, cataclysms of ecstasy, bliss down to their toes—and, when they returned, they were no longer afraid of death; yet they relished life even more. He wasn't sure he wanted to come that close. Besides, it wasn't death exactly that he was grappling with; it was the idea of death. Of autumn.

He reached the top of the hill. Leaves were strangely absent on the other side of the hill. Then he saw, at the bottom of the hill, a great heap of dried leaves. Children had gathered them into one magnificent pile, so they could leap into it.

He was a practical, skeptical, scientific man. Yet he was open-minded. Years ago, like his students, he had read Castañeda. The Indian sorcerer had advised Castañeda to keep death over his left shoulder. Or was it the right? And was that different from death breathing down your neck?

Take each breath as if it's your last—some mystical tradition, he couldn't recall which, advised that. Or did they say to breathe as if it were one's first breath? He took a deep breath. That was my last breath, he said to himself.

That was depressing.

He imagined his next breath was his first.

Millions of breaths to look forward to. Autumn to look forward to. He kept breathing, gasping his life, in and out. It made him dizzy, light-headed. Was he having a mystical experience?

No, he was hyperventilating.

Still, how many mystical infusions had he rejected because he had explained them away?

On the other hand, from all his reading, it seemed that you could not mistake a true mystical experience. The real thing, it was clear, grabbed you by the nape of the neck and shook you until you believed it.

Was he too old now for a mystical experience? They tended to hit in the mid-thirties. Jesus died at thirty-three. Dante was thirty-five when he got lost in the dark wood. Gopi Krishna was thirty-five when his kundalini popped up his spine and blew his mind into another dimension. During *his* thirty-fifth year—nine years had passed since then—he had waited, with anticipation, for the universe to smack *him* into cosmic consciousness.

It never happened.

He wasn't altogether sorry. The thing was scary, really. Turned you upside down. Made you a vegetarian.

It would have brought a lot of problems, and he didn't need more problems.

Of course, a mystical experience in the autumn of one's life was not impossible—no more than winning the powerball or escaping prostate trouble or falling in love was impossible. They just weren't likely.

In the past, whenever he had fallen in love, it had gotten him in trouble. There was the student, the hippie girl who wore combat boots and no bra, ten—was it twelve?—years ago. There was the Flemish woman, raven-haired and a practitioner of homeopathy, he met on his sabbatical in Europe. There was the new woman in the department, a deconstructionist who liked to be tied up, a mere two years ago. Trouble, every one of them. Complications. Discoveries. Jealousies. Scenes. Tears.

Affairs were simply too much trouble. Like the garden—an annual labor, a seasonal duty: you rent the rototiller; you plant, water, weed; you suffer the ravages of gophers, rabbits, hail; and at the end you have a zucchini the size of a cannon. Affairs were like that. A lot of work, and then, at harvest time, there's more than you can handle. Rapture turns against you. Everything's out of control.

Everything seemed to wash over him—marriage, affairs, children, tenure, committees, classes, tax returns—an ocean of time and events he was drowning in.

He took a deep breath and wondered if it was a first breath or a last. Or if he should even be breathing while he was drowning.

The Sufis talked about the "mother breath"—seven beats for the inhalation, hold for one, seven beats for the exhalation, hold for one, and repeat.

He tried it.

10

He wondered how fast he was supposed to count.

There was always something they didn't tell you.

Maybe he would become a Sufi. He wasn't sure where he should go. Turkey, maybe, but the political situation there was unstable. He was always wanting to go somewhere and become something after reading a book. After reading the first Castañeda book, he had gotten out a map of Mexico and wondered if he could find Don Juan and become his apprentice. He was going to spend a year in a Zen monastery. He wanted to study dolphins with John Lilly. He tried to change the oil in his car after reading *Zen and the Art of Motorcycle Maintenance.*

So it wasn't that he never tried to put his reading into practice. It was that things never worked out. Sitting cross-legged, trying *zazen* on his own, made his knees hurt; he limped for a week. He watched *Lila and Yoga*—or whatever it was called—on the educational channel, but one of the *asanas* had triggered his lower back pain, and for weeks afterward he had popped muscle relaxants. And, of course, driving to Mexico was absurd. No one knew if Don Juan even existed; besides, he had his classes to teach, and he couldn't afford it, anyway, what with the girls' dancing lessons, his teenage son's car insurance, and his wife's tuition for graduate school in psychology.

He looked down at the huge pile of leaves. The sun had set. The park was still deserted, except for him and the squirrels. The Sufis, he remembered, spun. He crossed his arms over his chest, as the dervishes did, and he turned counterclockwise, as they did.

He had read a story once about the Sufis who were

praying and chanting and spinning in a certain mosque in a village somewhere in the world; after they had prayed and chanted and spun for a long time, the room seemed ready to explode. Universal enlightenment seemed at hand. But then the sheik brought the dancing and chanting to a lower pitch, slowed it down, brought everyone back to earth. A visitor, disturbed, heartbroken, disappointed, asked the sheik, Why?—Why stop, when they were almost *there?* Because, the sheik answered, not everyone in the mosque was ready for enlightenment. And if you're not ready, enlightenment can destroy you. We wait, even the most advanced, until everyone is ready. Then, together, we will become one with the universe.

Spinning faster, he felt as if a thin wire were humming up and down his spine. He was losing himself in the spinning. He knew nothing, thought nothing, was nothing.

The wire broke. Dizziness picked him up by the heels and threw him down the hill.

He was rolling. He was in the leaves, covered, buried, drowning. He was laughing, picking the leaves out of his mouth.

He stood up, dizzy still. He didn't try to brush the leaves off. He couldn't find his cap. He ran unsteadily up the hill, turned, stood a moment—he could barely see the mound of leaves in the gathering darkness—then flung himself onto the earth and rolled, rolled, rolled—into the leaves again, the dry leaves crackling like little firecrackers, like sparks of electricity, like a loud rush of language from another dimension.

Over and over he ran up the hill, he rolled down, he

swam in the ocean of leaves—he lost his shoe—he didn't care—he lost his keys—he didn't care—he was losing his mind—good—until, finally, exhausted, breathless, sightless in the dark, he lay spread-eagled on the now flattened and scattered leaves. He couldn't have told who he was. He was lost. He was a goner. He was as crazy as a loon and he didn't care. His heels drummed the ground. He barked like a coyote. He howled like a wolf. He loosed his Tarzan yell, dormant these thirty years.

He walked—hobbled, actually, because he never found his shoe—the six blocks to his home. Leaves covered him like a costume, a motley, like the Sufis and other fools wore. He climbed his front steps. He could see into his living room, see his family watching television. He smelled like leaves. He reeked of autumn. It was in his hair and in his socks and under his collar. But he liked feeling that dusty, scratchy residue. He opened the door. He entered his house. He was grinning. He was breathing the mother breath. One-two-three-four-five-six-seven-hold-seven-six-five-four-three-two-one-hold—repeat.

They were grinning back at him.

Repeat.

Nearing Menopause, I Run into Elvis at Shoprite
Barbara Crooker

near the peanut butter. He calls me ma'am,
    like the sweet
southern mother's boy he was. This is the young Elvis,
slim-hipped, dressed in leather, black hair swirled
like a duck's backside. I'm in the middle of my life,
the start of the body's cruel betrayals, the skin beginning
to break in lines and creases, the thickening midline.
I feel my temperature rising, as a hot flash washes over,
the thermostat broken down. The first time I heard Elvis
on the radio, I was poised between girlhood
    and what comes next.
My parents were appalled, in the Eisenhower fifties,
    by rock
and roll and all it stood for, let me only buy one record,
"Love Me Tender," and I did.
I have on a tight Orlon sweater, circle skirt,
eight layers of rolled-up net petticoats, all bound
together by a woven straw cinch belt. Now I've come
full circle, hate the music my daughter loves, Nine
Inch Nails, Smashing Pumpkins, Crash Test Dummies.
Elvis looks embarrassed for me. His soft full lips
are like moon pies, his eyelids half-mast, pulled
down bedroom shades. He mumbles, "Treat me nice."

Now, poised between menopause and what comes next,
        the last
dance, I find myself in tears by the toilet paper rolls,
hearing "Unchained Melody" on the sound system. That's
all right now, Mama," Elvis says, "Any way you do is fine."
        The bass
line thumps and grinds, the honky-tonk piano moves
        like an ivory
river, full of swampy delta blues. And Elvis's voice
        wails above
it all, the purr and growl, the snarl and twang,
        above the chains
of flesh and time.

The Man Who Loved the Woman Who Loved Elvis
Terry Amrhein Tappouni

Buck Wallis wore his pompadour
high and glistening black,
a perfect downy ducktail
nestling against his neck.
Summers he sweltered down
in Florida, his imitation
leather jacket sticking
to him like plastic wrap
on pudding, knowing all
the time it wasn't enough.

The woman he loved still
slept with a velvet Elvis
on the wall above the foot
of her bed, slept on her back
so whenever her eyes opened
they would light on him,
his plush face aglow with
light from the hall, ripe
plum lips slightly open,
tugged up on one side.
People stared, slid contempt-
filled looks at the twenty-eight-
year-old man with the woman
who was turning fifty, even though

they said she looked good
for her age. The way he smiled
at her annoyed them in ways
they didn't understand. Men pulled
back their shoulders, felt
the yearning of their women.

What he knew was simple.
When "Love Me Tender" spilled
from the record player, and she
took him to her bed,
he was The King.

To the Husband Who Stands at the Sink, Intent on Shaving

Cortney Davis

There is a woman in your shower,
her body visible through the green
canopy of steam. She isn't as young
as she used to be, but you've said
you hardly notice. Now her dark hair
cleaves to her neck like leaves
and beads of water decorate her skin,
slide opal and diamond bracelets down
the blood flush raised by heat.
Everyday she walks or lifts weights,
praising the way thighs tighten,
how muscles rise and divide her back
into twin slices of fruit—sweet,
succulent, firm against the lip.
Now she admires the long arm she raises
to direct the spray against her breasts;
have you looked away from the mirror
to watch? In case you have, she turns,
giving you freely her profile, this map
of the body complete with betrayals
slightly hidden behind the wavering glass.

One hand ringed in gold
slowly approaches the faucet. Languid,
wide-awake, she prepares to emerge
like a water bird slipping from water
into air, feathers slicked, stripped clean
of anger and sorrow, not yet of expectation.

At the Reunion
Mark DeFoe

Blundering from our own lifeboats, we clench
flesh thought lost, backslap and hug, flash snapshots
of kids, those blessed torments of love, parade
the new wife with the tight thighs. Giddy with
survivor bravado, we puff our jobs,
kite our incomes, balloon our travel plans,
add wings to the old hacienda.

We search out the one who understood us then,
lock secret fingers, sway in the spell
of golden oldies. Smoky dreams slow dance
through the crowd like a tipsy magician,
vanishing bald spot and crows-feet.

Ah, we croon old tunes, losing not one word,
each moment grand cliché, but completely ours,
the sexiest, classiest class of all.

We toast the shades who have passed, touch glasses
and believe. Around us are those who knew
us when. In their eyes we meet the boy
who dropped the pass that lost The Game,
the girl almost runner-up for May Queen.

And yet a gleam of sweetness there, that allows
again the tender seed of self that was.
Let the band play on, corny as they are.
Take my hand. For this last dance we have returned.

Illusions
Michael S. Glaser

With age, with reluctance,
I lose my illusions,

look back on those sweet desires
I imagined as prize,

as though I knew
what I was being drawn into.

Only late am I learning
what attention must be paid

and how help comes
not to blaze a path of light

but to sustain our faltering steps,
to see us through the night.

Reflections in Green Glass
Davi Walders

For C., J., and all brave women who love

Too early to be fashionable, two women perch
on stools eating *ensalada,* our faces reflected
in the glass above the bar, our backs a partition
between Catalan, coffee, and laughter. It is dusk
in Barcelona. Waiters balancing *tapas* high
in smoky air tell us what we already know.

We are out of sync, but we have taken a stand
to sit at the bar because of our feet,
our stomachs, and our desires. We will not eat
again at midnight to lie bedded in our bloat,
staring into darkness, deprived of dreams
by dinner and aging bodies that will not adjust.

We lean, tired, looking into milky green glass.
Longer than Liceu's curtain, it shimmers like rain
on old copper, encircling Picadillos on the *passeig.*
Beveled shelves, triangles of herb brandy, Chartreuse
and necks of rioja bottles frame our silhouettes.
We are women beyond the blur of crowded tables.

Two women, dining too early, happy to be out
of the rain, damp feet warming on zinc, we talk
of friends at fifty who buy answering machines,
wait for calls, keep money hidden in drawers, open
separate accounts, begin and end careers, take lovers,
let them go, reweave, unravel, gather and lose,
tighten and loosen their hold on children, thighs,
lies, and fears. Reflections dancing in green glass,
out of sync, out of touch, out of the rain,
out of laughter, out of love for women walking
in the world—we raise our *vino blanco,* saluting,
drinking in the Spanish dusk, laughing at fifty.

photo by Robert Ullman

photo by Marianne Gontarz

Bountiful Harvest
Sally Whitney

Heat from the sun is warm against my neck as I bend over John's okra plants, looking for the fuzzy green spears that are the peak size, moments before they become large and tough. "Can't let 'em get too old," John says to me, as he has every summer of the twenty-five years we've been married. I shove my straw hat back on my head and glare at him, although he can't see me because he is tying up tomato plants that last night's rain pushed away from their stakes. The garden is John's comfort zone, the patch where when his hands are busy his tongue often loosens. So I follow him into the dirt and heat and bugs sometimes, to talk.

Today I want to talk about his birthday. In two weeks he'll be fifty years old, a milestone I consider worthy of celebration, but every time I mention it, he makes a joke and talks about something else. "So what do you want to do for your birthday?" I ask. I twist an okra stem until the pod falls into my basket.

"Can it," he says and throws a tomato at me. His curly hair with flecks of white in the curves is pressed under his stained leather cap, reminding me of an old-fashioned paperboy in a Norman Rockwell print. By reflex, my hand shoots out and stops the red pulp from splattering against the side of the house. I grimace at his pun. What I really want to do is give him a surprise party, but I'm afraid he'll be angry, or at least unhappy, if I do. I can't tell for sure how he feels.

"How about going out for dinner? Or maybe a few friends over?"

"Don't make a big deal." His head is back down in the tomatoes, and I am staring at his derriere, still as slim and sexy as ever in his soft denim jeans. I sigh and pull off an okra that is hardly as big as my thumb.

The next day my sister comes by to return a book she borrowed. Her name is Alicia, and she is a compulsive dropper inner. "Any decision on the birthday bash?" she asks. She knows my dilemma and is unsympathetic. Her husband Martin loves parties and is only forty-five, anyway.

"Not an inkling." I throw my Pledge-soaked dustrag on the table and wipe my hands on my jeans.

"I'm telling you, Judy, just do it. He'll love it." Alicia goes to my refrigerator, takes out two Diet Cokes, and hands one to me. "Sit down and let me tell you about men." This is my younger sister who thinks she knows more about the opposite sex than I do. Grateful for any excuse to stop cleaning, however, I sit. "Where is John now?" Alicia asks.

"At the grocery store getting something for dinner."

"Is he cooking again?"

"I thought you were going to tell me about men."

"He wants you to think he doesn't want to be fussed over, but he does."

"I'm not sure." I remember his face at his last birthday. He smiled as our daughters, home from college, gave him a candle-covered cake, but it wasn't a real smile. A real smile brightens his pale eyes and sparkles in the corners of his face. This smile said, "I'm glad you want to make me happy and I'll try to make you think you did."

"Then what does he want?"

"I think he wants to pretend he's not getting older."

"Kind of hard to deny, isn't it?" Alicia sips her Coke and curls her legs under her on the couch. The air conditioner hums in the window, but I am still warm from dusting. I hold my Coke can against my cheek.

"Why is it that somewhere in life, getting older becomes bad?" I hope Alicia doesn't think I'm being trite. If she does, she doesn't show it. "I can remember when I thought twelve must be the most wonderful age in the world. And then I wanted to be sixteen so I could drive, and twenty-one so I could drink, and even thirty was nice because I figured by that time, I was truly an adult."

Alicia turns and stretches her legs in front of her. She looks more interested. "How about forty? Did you really want to be forty?"

I think back to that time in my life. "Yeah. I did. I spent my thirties staying up with babies and chasing after little kids. By forty, my life settled down. I had more time to think about me."

"But you don't want to be fifty any more than John does."

She is looking directly at me now, her face an expression of challenge she has used on me since she was five. I don't feel challenged.

"They say at fifty you earn the name 'wise old woman.'

I think I'll like that."

Alicia laughs, steadying her Coke can with both hands. "That's what I'll call you, Judy," she says between laughs, "wise old woman. My wise old sister. Sort of like an owl."

"Who's like an owl?" John appears at the kitchen door, his arms wrapped around bulging sacks of groceries. He is wearing a white T-shirt with illustrations of endangered species front and back. A polar bear protrudes slightly over his belt.

Alicia composes herself and points her finger at me. "Your wife," she says. "Hadn't you noticed?"

"Stays up all night and sleeps all day." John grins in my direction.

"Get out of here, both of you," I say.

"I do have to go." Alicia stands and carries her Coke can to the kitchen. "Thanks for the book and remember what I said about the other thing." Her words trail her as she passes through again on her way out the front door.

"What other thing?" John sets the sacks on the kitchen counter, pulls out a box of cereal, and puts it on the top shelf next to the rice, raisins, peanut butter. Always the same order. Once I tried to put tea bags between the rice and raisins. John was grumpy all day.

He is looking at me now, one eyebrow cocked like a question mark. I put my arms around his waist and lay my head against his chest. He smells like bananas and Brute. "She's talking about your birthday," I say. "We want to do something big."

"I'm big enough already." John chuckles and gently pushes me away. There is no mirth in his laugh. "Besides, it's not a big deal."

"I think it is." Suddenly, I'm tired of dancing around the issue. "I think when a person achieves fifty years of life, that's something to be proud of, an accomplishment."

John folds a paper bag methodically, smoothing each crease between his fingers. His cheeks droop. "That's the problem, Judy," he says. "I don't have the accomplishment I wanted." He is quiet for a few minutes, and I wait. When he is ready, he goes on. "I've worked for the same company for twenty years. I've been an engineer, a technical specialist, a department manager, and a division manager. I thought by the time I was fifty, I'd be a vice president. It's a goal I set for myself, and I failed." He shrugs and goes back to folding the bag.

I have raised two daughters, cared for my mother when she was sick, and reached out to lots of friends in need, but I don't remember ever experiencing the pain of compassion that I feel now. I go to him again, and this time he doesn't push me away.

In the darkness that night, I stare at the ceiling and listen to John's rough breathing beside me. His in-and-out rhythm of air matches the tug-of-war in my mind. As he slips into deeper sleep, I know what I will do.

"Come help me," I say to Alicia on the phone the next morning. "I need your creative flair."

"No long guest list?" she asks when I tell her my plan.

"No long guest list." I'm sure.

The morning of John's birthday is cool with low-hanging clouds. I give him a Shoebox card at breakfast so he leaves for work with at least a hint of a smile. At 10:00 A.M. I cross

31

my fingers and hope that the roses I ordered are delivered to his office on time.

After work, I hurry home to make sure everything is ready by the time John gets home. Alicia arrives at 4:30, Martin shows up at 5:00, and by 5:30 we are set. We turn off the lights, close the shades, and, giggling like children, hide behind the living room furniture. Very slowly, the door knob begins to turn. I hold my breath to stop my giggling and watch the wedge of light pour through the widening crack of the door. As John steps across the threshold, I throw the switch controlling the outlet to which Alicia and I have painstakingly wired every light in the room as well as our ancient slide projector.

"Surprise!" we yell. The lights form a halo for the life-size image of John projected against the rear living room wall.

"Happy birthday to you," we sing at the top of our lungs while we clasp hands and dance in a ring around John, who looks dazed.

"Right this way," I say, and lead John to the dining room, where we have taken down the Andrew Wyeth prints that usually hang there and replaced them with blown-up pictures of John—John with our daughters when they were little, John hanging our fragile Christmas star, John with his dad and brothers at Thanksgiving.

"What is this?" John asks, but there's no anger in his voice. I seat him at the head of the dining room table and hold his hand while Alicia and Martin begin a slow procession from the kitchen carrying a two feet-by-four feet sheet cake slathered in lemon icing. They place it on the table in front of John, and he stares at it a full minute before he says, "Those aren't candles."

Stuck in the mounds of icing are an array of figurines, objects, and small photographs, each with a tag attached. John lifts a porcelain cocker spaniel out of a yellow drift and reads his card aloud, "This is for the time you pulled Corky out of the river and saved his life." John nods and licks the icing from the pooch's feet.

"Look at this one." Alicia grabs a red sedan and thrusts it at John.

"This is for the time you cosigned Alicia's car loan when we all thought she couldn't keep a job more than six months." John laughs and Alicia kisses his cheek.

The phone rings as John reaches for a plastic suitcase. I answer it and hand it to John. He pauses, then says, "Yeah, I have the cake right here. Which one? OK." He lifts a blue book labeled "Chemistry" out of the icing, studies the card, and smiles. "You could have passed it by yourself." He talks a while longer, then hands me the phone. "It was Deborah," he says. I nod, knowing our other daughter will call soon.

"I don't understand all this," John says, his eyebrows curving.

"We're celebrating who you are," I explain, "the person you've become in fifty years." Alicia, Martin, and I join John at the table now, cheering as he lifts each item, licks the icing from its base, and sets it in a row next to the cake. The row grows long, an army of testaments ready to do battle for John. John is smiling, not a pretend smile to make us feel good, but a real smile that spreads from his hairline to his chin.

"Oh, come on, Judy. This is too much," he says as he pulls a long green okra from the icing.

"That stands for the magnificent gardens you produce year after year." I pat his arm as he examines the pod.

"But it's too tough to eat," John says.

"It's not here to be dinner," I say. "It's here because it's big like your heart."

Fathers Playing Sons
Robert L. Harrison

Challenged by youth, we played that day
like reflections in the mirror.
Old skills come back, but muscles don't
as our limbs defy our minds.

This game we played like pros of old
staring down at endless motion,
bringing in our belts a notch while
mentally melting our excess weight.

Ninety feet was still the same
but our glasses made it longer,
and our fastest was not as swift
compared to their sneaker dust.

But wisdom, I thought, was on our side
as I made a brilliant bunt,
only to have the ball die of age
and scar my back forever.

And I pitched like slo-mo Ryan
wheezing only a little, as my best
went straight down the pike
only to fly back into uncharted skies.

We tied the score between youth and age
and stopped only because of darkness.
We celebrated with good grace but knew
the future would catch us napping.

For they had keen eyes and miracle legs
and a knack for coming back,
but we ancient ones will never quit
for fathers must always beat their sons.

photo by Teresa Tamura

photo by Bayla Winters

Hands
Michael Andrews

This year my hands turned old.

I can see the grief in them—
the scars, of course, stand out
skin flayed by knives and glass and bites
and the blisters big as half dollars
ripped from the calluses by the high bar
and the shovels and axes and hammers
shaping the earth,
but the earth always wins.

I can see the wars in them
Vietnam and Iran and Nicaragua and Bangladesh.
I can see the years of poverty
the inability to get published.
I can see Flo's cancer
and my blackouts
and all the creditors
and promises lost.

I can see the victories in them
small
and mixed with little scars.

The nails have turned to ridges,
each one a plowed field
waiting for a harvest that will never come.
They were never strong, but my hands are.
They are big and they are kind.
I guess they could be described as capable hands.

They have made so many things.
I used them to shape wood and books
to sculpture a poem and print a picture.
They have done their share of plumbing
and automobile mechanics, electrical wiring
and, yes, squeezing triggers.

They are coarse hands, but they are gentle.
They are magic for cat's ears
and dog's rumps and tickling children.
They are healers too.
They can rub the pain away
the fear
and the tears.

They can make love.

I saw them change early in the spring.
I thought it was darkroom chemicals,
the gasoline and the lacquer thinner.

I saw the skin go leather
textured and knobby
with rivers of wrinkles and lines
and five years of hard living.
I rubbed them with enough grease to pack an axle.
Not a single hand cream worked as advertised.
I changed detergents.
Nothing helped.

Driving into L.A. on the Harbor Freeway
my hands were caught in that fierce
morning sun
and they were old.

These days
when they have nothing to do
they are hiding in my pockets
or laying in the shade.

Still,
they are big and clumsy and friendly.

The kind of hands that brush tears away.

Aerodynamic Integrity
Rose Hamilton-Gottlieb

I meet my two friends, Mag and Addie, at Bill's Bike Shop. Addie climbs onto a flimsy-looking contraption and uses the kickstand for balance. She looks at home there. Her bones are as delicate as the fingers of chrome that hold the bicycle together, and her hair curves over her cheeks like silver crescent moons.

"Racing bikes. That's what you need for a ride like that." The salesman is a college jock type with a blond crewcut.

"It's not a race." Mag eyes the bicycles with mistrust.

Addie has challenged us to ride across her native state of Iowa on an annual odyssey sponsored by the Des Moines Register. A native of Southern California who's never seen any reason to land anywhere east of the Rockies, I don't seriously think we will do this. But my thighs could use a little trimming. And I'm ready for something.

The salesman doesn't even look at Mag, who leans toward me and whispers, "See what I mean, Sally? He doesn't even see me."

At our last book club meeting, Mag said, "What I fear most is becoming like the old lady..."

"Elderly woman," I corrected.

"The elderly woman you almost run down in the supermarket before you realize she's there. You know, the one the waiter never asks if everything is OK?" We were discussing Germaine Greer's *The Change* since we're all experiencing menopause in one form or another, and truth to tell, have been experiencing it all our lives in the sometimes whispered, sometimes ridiculed, always feared, idea of it.

"Don't be paranoid," I say now, but Crew Cut relates only to Addie, who nobody ignores. He wheels out a metallic red space-age contraption and pats the narrow seat. "You want something light. Slim tires. Low handlebars. Something with aerodynamic integrity."

"With what?" I ask.

Addie climbs on and curves herself over the handlebars. "See how the wind will flow over my head?"

"Isn't that a boy's bike?" I look for my childhood bicycle, one with a frame designed to protect a young girl's virginity, embarrassed to admit that the last bike I rode required the rider to pedal backward in order to stop.

Mag peers through tortoise shell-framed glasses at the complicated system of wires looped over the handlebars. "Are all those gears necessary?"

"You need gears. Lots of them."

Twenty-one gears in all. We start at my house and pedal down the bike lane. Our maiden voyage, Mag calls it, but it's not clear sailing. We teeter dangerously on the skinny tires, off-balance, weaving over the line, not sure of the gears. My hair creeps from under the helmet into my eyes, but I'm afraid to let go of the handlebars long enough to push it back.

My hair was another germaine topic at our last book club meeting. I was complaining to Mag that my hairdresser had tried to sell me on a tint. "It's this in-between stage I hate," I lied. "Actually, I look forward to being a...a...a..." I couldn't think of a word to replace *brunette* on my driver's license.

"Greyhead?" Mag asked dryly.

"Seriously, don't you think I'll look good in grey? I mean with my summer coloring?" Trying to warm to the idea, I added, "Maybe I'll hurry things along by covering what's left of the brown."

"To dye or not to dye. That is the question." Mag ran her hand through her pageboy, once silky chestnut, now streaked with coarse silver.

Addie slammed her hand down onto the table and said, "I challenge you." Since Addie's own hair had turned a stunning shade of pewter in her early thirties, she was understandably bored with the conversation. And, since Addie's challenges are hard to ignore, here we are.

"Watch it, Sally," Addie shouts, too late. I clip her back fender. With my back curved into a widow's hump and my hands at the level of my knees like some missing link, I can't see more than a foot beyond the front tire, and every time I raise my head to enjoy the smogless January sky, I swerve out of control.

Back home, I untangle myself from the instrument of torture. My neck is stiff, my wrists ache, my back hurts, and the narrow seat may have done permanent damage to parts I hope I'm not through using yet. I chuck off the helmet and glimpse in the window, hair matted with sweat. "If this is supposed to make me feel young, it's not working."

"You need a haircut," Addie says.

"No, I need new friends."

Mag careens into the driveway, falls off, then limps to where I've collapsed on the front step. "That was very nice, Addie," she says, ever the diplomat and mediator, "but Sally and I need different bikes."

Back at the bike shop, Crew Cut says, "You need a hybrid, a cross between a mountain bike and a street bike. Stay with the lighter frame but get touring-style handlebars. Keep the smooth tread but get wider tires for balance."

"And a bigger seat," I put in. He ignores me.

"Of course you'll lose up to four miles an hour." He shakes his head.

"It's not a race," Mag says firmly.

Addie trades in hers too, then insists we buy biking pants, the fashion crime of the century, in my opinion. I'm sold, finally, by the padding in the seat, but we resist the sales pitch on skin-tight jerseys and opt for thigh-length T-shirts.

"I'll design a logo," Mag volunteers.

I knew Mag couldn't be trusted. Her logo is a picture of Baba Yaga on her broomstick. Obese, greasy haired, snaggle toothed. (Last summer we read *Women Who Run with the Wolves*.) And beneath this slimy old hag, the words, "The Three Crones." In-your-face-we're-old-so-what.

Mag, who's into goddess stories and myths and Jungian psychology, responded to Addie's challenge with, "You know, this might fulfill a need we read about; that is, the lack of ritual in our culture to mark the transition period between youth and old age. Like a rite of passage into a golden age filled with possibilities and adventure."

"In Iowa?" I asked.

Addie, who knows when to encourage Mag, said, "Oh there's lots of ritual. True believers dip their back wheels in the Missouri at the beginning of the week and their front wheels in the Mississippi at the end."

"Perfect." Mag clapped her hands. "It's rife with symbolism."

All that talk about water reminded me that my bladder is in need of repair—my last shred of argument. "What about bathrooms?"

"Ever hear of cornfields?" Addie quipped, then quickly added, "From what I hear, the Porta-Potti concession cleans up at the ride."

We each order two of Mag's T-shirts, but I wear mine fraudulently, secretly ashamed of getting old.

After six months of Addie's relentless training, we ride fifty miles in one day. Addie says with the group energy supplied by ten thousand bikers, we'll easily do the required sixty- to eighty-mile days.

I get a haircut.

"My, look at all that grey on the floor," my hairdresser comments tactlessly.

I look down at the last of my former brunette status.

"How about a little tint? I had a cancellation."

I'm tempted. "How long will it take?"

"About an hour. Make that two hours if you add a cellophane treatment to lock in the color."

I check my watch. I still have twenty-five miles to ride before it gets dark, and in spite of my old hair, my muscles yearn for action.

"Next time," I say.

For Addie and Mag and me, the ride starts a day early, at the mosquito-infested junction of the Rock and Big Sioux Rivers, which forms the border between Iowa and South Dakota. We have pedaled the fifteen miles from our motel in Sioux Center to dip our back tires in this tributary of the Missouri. I was for not doing this part and saying we did, but Mag insists we need all the ritual we can get.

We dip our tires and pedal back through the deepening twilight. I feel the strength in my legs and in my lungs and in our friendship. "Thanks for making me do this. I could go across the whole state tonight."

Addie lifts her arms and embraces the evening. "A piece of cake."

We meet a few other purists, including two young men who pass us on the way back, balancing a bucket of river water between them. "What on earth?" Mag asks.

"It's for our buddies. We drew the short straws; they get to drink beer."

"That's cheating," Addie calls out, but they've left us behind, the full bucket perfectly balanced between their racing bikes.

At the motel, we wash our clothes, put on our one change, which we will sleep in tonight and ride in tomorrow, and take in performances by the Senior Citizen Kitchen Band, a local ventriloquist, and the country comedy team of "Ezra and Lubas." We play "cow bingo" and observe a hay-bale stacking contest at the fairgrounds and watch this town of five thousand swell to a colorful tent city. Most of the bikers are young, with every muscle and curve ensheathed in spandex.

At Sunday's opening ceremony, the mayor's speech includes the weather report: "Sunshine, with highs in the seventies. Wind five to ten miles an hour in the northeast. That means a gentle tailwind. I checked the topography maps," he says, "and the good news is that it's 749 feet downhill from here to Burlington. The bad news is that it's 495 miles."

"Anyone for a head start?" Mag says.

We leave before the National Anthem and set out into the Iowa dawn, three abreast, cornfields on both sides of the two-lane highway, which has been closed to traffic. Our destination is Spencer, sixty-one miles, a paltry distance for veteran bikers such as we.

We travel light with one clean set of clothes, a plastic raincoat, a toothbrush, and hormone replacement pills. Mag is on my left, Addie on my right. A few other early birds whiz past, but most of the bikers are waiting for the town fathers to dump a huge tub of river water across the starting line. Addie says it's to accommodate those without the integrity to do the real thing, and Mag says it's typically American fast-food ritual.

For the moment, we share the morning with only a red-winged blackbird, scolding us on the wing. "Look," I say, "a native Iowan wants to race," and I surge forward after the bird, feeling about ten years old. In my mirror, I see Mag and Addie laugh. "See you in Spencer," I call out. "Last one there buys the beer."

I pedal on alone, so engrossed in the morning I hardly notice a roar in the distance. I slow to let Mag and Addie catch up. From behind comes a young male voice, "On your left." Startled, I move to the right, only to hear another voice, this time female, "On your right." I glimpse creamy skin beneath wraparound sunglasses as she passes, so close I smell her bubblegum.

"Stay in your lane," she snaps, "or you'll cause an accident."

I open my mouth to tell her to get rid of the gum before she chokes on it, but am checked by another "On your left," followed by an "On your right." And another and another. I stare at the concrete ahead, not daring to even glance at the passing scenery lest I veer in either direction and get hit. I clench the handlebars, check my mirror for Addie and Mag, but they are gone. I almost collide with a man with a tattoo on his arm and more hair on his legs than I have on my head. "Sorry," I apologize, but he's out of earshot and another biker moves into his place, shows me the back of his T-shirt: "If you can't run with the big dogs, stay on the porch." I try to slow down, but I'm trapped in a fast-moving river of chrome and rubber and spandex-covered flesh. I fight panic. I've lost my friends.

The day stays cool, but my palms are slippery with sweat and anxiety threatens to choke off my breath. My legs itch from at least thirty mosquito bites. I struggle to keep up, but feel like a tangle of driftwood in swift water.

"Speed up, you old crone, or get out of the fast lane." Damn T-shirt.

"How?" I gasp, but the owner of the voice is already gone. I long, not for the slow lane, but to get off altogether. This was a mistake. I am too cautious. Too slow. Too old. Yet I pedal on as the hours go by.

Foolishly, I begin to cry. I look at my odometer. I have gone twenty-five miles and I'm tired. Every muscle hurts, not from pedaling, but from tension. I see myself swept along in terror until my heart gives out. I see my bicycle drop and unsuspecting bikers pile up in a chain reaction, not seeing me until it's too late. Like the old lady with the shopping cart.

I'm thirsty. Others tip water bottles at full speed, but I know my balance isn't good enough. The sun is straight up now, and humidity settles like dew on my already sweat-soaked body. I have to go to the bathroom.

"Rumbles!" A shout from up ahead. Bikers veer to the left and to the right, exposing a speed bump made of strips of concrete. Afraid to leave my lane, I bounce over it at full speed. My neck creaks, my teeth shake, my bladder leaks. I hear laughter and it makes me mad enough to demand, "On your left." It works, and I'm one lane over. Five more "On your lefts" and I pull off onto the shoulder.

I look at the flawless youth straining toward the next town, and the next, eyes on the pavement, shoulders hunched, bodies conforming perfectly to the laws of aerodynamics to maximize energy, save time, create speed, get there first to see who can drink the most beer. No thank you. I toss my bicycle in the ditch, grab the water bottle, and make for the cornfield.

I wade through head-high green leaves until I'm a million miles from the ride. I guzzle water. I pee. I drink and pee at the same time. Finished at last, I discover my knees are locked into a squatting position. An ugly grasshopper leaps at me, convinces me I can stand. I find a spot where the corn is thin and I lie down on the fragrant earth to sleep. Or die. I don't care which.

I awake looking up at the crones on Mag and Addie's T-shirts.

"We saw your bike," Mag says. "Are you OK?"

I'm about to resign when Addie says, "Wow, did you take off. We thought you'd be in Spencer by now. How's it feel to be a jock?"

"You mean joke."

"How long were you asleep?" Mag asks.

I look at my watch. "About an hour. You two just get here?"

"We just happened to see your bike. I thought we were going to stick together," Mag said, resentful now that it's obvious I haven't had a stroke.

I struggle to my feet and lead the way out of the corn-field, try to control my disappointment that my bike hasn't been stolen. "Look, I don't know if I can ride any more," I start to say, but Addie is still shaking her head in disbelief. "Do you realize how far ahead of us you were?"

I think. I was an hour ahead of them. I check my watch and odometer. I have ridden thirty miles in a little over two hours, on a treadmill my aging heart was not designed to endure. Yet it had endured. I realize something else. "I'm starved."

"Come on," Mag says, "I just saw a Sweet Corn for Sale Two Miles Ahead sign."

I get on my bike and follow, shaky and clinging to the rough shoulder of the road.

"On your left, honey." A grey ponytail beneath a scarlet

helmet, thighs of pure cellulite, a wrinkled face turned blissfully to the eastern horizon. She moves around me and in her place is a young man with a beard on an ancient touring bike with a sign, Gears Are for Wimps. A couple ride tandem, pulling a homemade cart with a sleeping child. Fifties music hits me like a shot of adrenaline as a teenager passes, a boom box on wheels in tow.

A pothole yawns before me, and I steel myself to change lanes. Palms sweating, I cry out, "On your right," and miraculously, a place opens up for me. "Thank you," I say to an elderly man on a recumbent bike who drifts by with his face turned upward to billowy clouds.

"You're quite welcome, young lady," he replies. Apparently, here at the end of the line, there's room for amenities.

A group of six comes along, dressed in black-and-white spotted jerseys with little rubber horns attached to their helmets. Cows. They laugh and call out to one another. A pink rubber swan behind a biker's seat. A kite attached to a fishing pole attached to handlebars. No one seems to care when they get to Spencer or if they get there at all. It's just like that annual spoof on the Tournament of Roses, the Doodah Parade. Everyone is having fun. I'm having fun. There's a conspicuous absence of spandex, and I wonder where all these people were last night. Why didn't I see them then?

I look at Mag on my left and Addie on my right. "A piece of cake," Addie says, just before they both swerve to avoid a speed bump. On purpose, I bounce over it and call out a warning to those who come after, "Ruuuummbbllesss." I hear my fragmented voice, like an old sheep baaing, and I laugh. Is that my laugh, that cackle floating over the corn-fields, or is it some ancient Baba Yaga riding on my back?

Once again I have left Mag and Addie behind, and I stop to let them catch up. I pull off my helmet to feel the breeze on my scalp, and in the mirror I catch sight of my silver hair. Above my blue eyes and summer skin, it looks good. I notice a turn in the road up ahead and I see thousands of bicycles curving with it, winding over the tender land, the sun flashing on beautiful chrome and metallic color. I move back into that Doodah Parade, and head downhill to the mighty Mississippi, a gentle wind at my back.

Nothing's Been the Same Since John Wayne Died

William Greenway

My world isn't hers, skin
like mocha coffee she climbs
into each morning, air pouring
through her throat clear
as creek water, no line where
brown legs slide into
silk shorts. She's my student
but I'm in class now, aerobics,
flunking in a room of convex
mirrors and dumbbells, though
she's patient, pities me, the
sounds I make for air. It's
hopeless as a dancing bear, Disney
hippo in a tutu, a friend's
father. She wants to pop
candy in my mouth when I do
something right. To her, cigarettes
smell like burning celery, liquor
is shellac, her heart has a slow
beat and sticks to it, she can bench press
me. I sort of pity her, daughter
I never had, how far she has
to go, how dirty and heavy.

But she's perfect now, and even
her hard music gets under my
fat, sets my frog legs jumping
in jeans stores.
She's working hard to get me young,
I'm aging her fast, and three times
a week we keep meeting here.

photo by Marianne Gontarz

Dance Class
Ann Cooper

Mothers and grandmothers,
we coax our morning muscles
and contort our arthritic toes,
cavorting to throbbing rhythms.
Never mind the beanpole teacher,
younger than our daughters,
who shouts steps and encouragement
and knows she'll never be that old.

Humor is our sustaining virtue.
No pain, no gain, we laugh,
tight thighs are the prize,
grateful we can undertake
routine maintenance for our
sagging, high-mileage bodies.

Inside we are graceful, slim,
and young—recollecting jeté,
plié, and grand battement;
floating in gossamer gowns
across Swan Lake landscapes.
Glimpses in the mirrored wall
show us our lissome body myths.
We are immune to absurdity.

Small boys pass the windows,
grinning. We clown for them—
parody bad backs, pull faces,
confirm their preconceptions
with proof of weird and agéd.
We are witches and doubt not
that stiff, wrinkled, and old
beats the sole alternative.

photo by Roger Pfingston

Getting Older
Jane Aaron Vander Wal

no longer will I try to impersonate youth
cancel my facial with the surgeon's blade
let the wind and sun erode
aging tissue fascinates me

no longer a brittle walking bush am I
my hair shall grow long straight and grey
catching insects for its food
scorning the hairdresser's chemistry

exercise class memories fade fast
into the toes of discarded running shoes
I shall move only when sunlight sucks me out of my chair
anointing my walks
and causing me to bend down over short flowers

Bonuses
Dori Appel

The monthly service charge
has vanished like magic
from my bank statement.
It's because I'm fifty-five,
and it's only the beginning!
In five more years the food co-op
will discount all my groceries,
and in another five I'll qualify for
social security, bargain movies,
vacations at special rates.
Airlines will reduce their fares,
then call my name for early boarding,
the drugstore will fill prescriptions
minus ten per cent, and eventually
the newspaper will send
a deferential young reporter
to take down my advice on life.
Finally, when I am as dry and light
as a dragonfly's wing
and no longer satisfied with
mere discounts and reductions,
I'll slip out quietly,
absolutely free.

Queen of Cards and Powders
William Ratner

It is Sunday, and Saspi is waiting for a man. She has been waiting for two weeks. He works across the street at night as a greeter at Carmelita's L.A. Salsa Club and Dinner House. He is Armenian, but the waiters and parking attendants call him the Cubano because of his pencil mustache, his neatly tailored linen suits, and the fact that he speaks a rapid Spanish like a Cuban. The Cubano sleeps during the afternoons and wakes at dusk to prepare for work as the greeter. But on Sundays he rises early. He stops at Saspi's store to buy cigarettes, and he walks alone to St. Mary's Armenian Apostolic Church.

Saspi sits behind her counter at the International European Delicatessen on Vermont Avenue, surrounded by the fragrance of crushed mint and the sumac, paprika, and sesame on the Armenian pizza and *tahin* bread she can no longer eat. She has just turned sixty, and Dr. Sarkis tells her that fat is her enemy.

It was exactly two Sundays ago that the Cubano caught hold of Saspi's wrist as she handed him his cigarettes. She stared at his thin, umber face, his eyes shaded by thick brows. He smelled of lime and honey. With callused fingers and the elegance of an older man he stroked her palm, white as eggshell. They stood like this for some time, drifting between softened breaths. Then the Cubano withdrew his hand, and saying nothing, he left.

Saspi dresses by her mirror and thinks of the firm cut of his jaw. She wants to place her hands there. She dreams of being with the Cubano, lying with him in straw, in sunlight.

She hopes that her friend Maria Theresa will not ask again if the Cubano has come for his cigarettes. She has decorated this poor man with so many lies. This morning in the store she tells Saspi, "He screamed out your name in his apartment last night. I swear to la Virgin. It woke me. He was up there pacing like a wolf. He broke a glass too, probably a blood ritual to win you. He worships you, Saspi. I saw him take a picture of you with his Instamatic. Don't let him down. Ah, to hell with him, don't let me down. I've put a lot of hope into this, girl. I have a friend from the botanica I'm going to bring over. She can help get you the Cubano."

Soon Saspi will walk the half mile to St. Mary's in hopes of seeing him. This makes her want to eat. She eyes the tins of baklava and raisin cookies and sips her coffee. Coffee has become her pleasure. She has rearranged the shelves so that the Plexiglas bins of coffee beans are closer to her, and she can reach in and stir them with her fingers and smell the sooty black Turk Kahva she imports to make the little cups of Armenian coffee for her customers—old men who claim her coffee gives them renewed sexual prowess, immigrants who crowd around the cash register and discuss the Armenian earthquake, churchgoers who boast about their grandsons and drop coins into the plastic donation box on the counter for the children of

Armenia and Karabagh.

Dr. Sarkis walks through the door. His suit coat is always buttoned even on the hottest days, and he carries his backgammon board—a tiny attaché case covered in scuffed tawny leather with burnished hinges. He opens it and fingers the round wooden game pieces as if touching a lover.

"You seem disappointed, Saspi. Were you expecting someone else? You're dressed like you're going to a wedding."

"I'm closing up soon. I'm going to church."

The doctor feigns a shocked expression. "Did an archangel come to you in your sleep? What about your customers?"

"They can get coffee over at McDonald's."

"The Sunday brunch at church is fatty, Saspi."

"I'm not going there to eat."

"Why are you going?"

Saspi glances at the avenue. Mist is burning off under the midmorning August sun. Rusted white security gates are stretched across the front of Carmelita's. She is weary of Dr. Sarkis. He proposed marriage to her over a year ago and only a month after his wife died. Saspi suspects the woman probably expired from all the cleaning, polishing, and laundering he required of her.

"I'm going to hear my sister sing in the choir, Doctor."

"Nahreen's been singing in that choir forever."

"So she's had time to get good; I should hear her sing."

Saspi steps behind the deli case and busies herself preparing the doctor's cup of coffee.

"Be sure not to stir it, Saspi; you'll disturb the sediment."

She removes the stainless steel cezve from the flame and pours the sugary black liquid into his cup. When Saspi was a child her mother told her that the best weapon against a lecture from a man is silence, not the silence of obeisance but simply to ignore him in the hope that his need to commandeer the ship, as she put it, might subside. Passing sixty means that Saspi will probably have to endure even more lectures about blood sugar, fat-to-muscle ratio, the chastity of older women.

Saspi's husband, Seto, has been dead for nineteen years, yet the memory of his lectures is as fresh as the headache that has begun to fill her brow. Seto gave advice until the day he died of prostate cancer at age fifty-one. In a small double room at Queen of Angels Hospital, with plastic tubes taped to his nose, liquids dripping into bruised punctures, he declared, "The store must be free of clutter, or the business will evaporate like tea in the desert."

Seto was like a Chinese fortune cookie; open him up and there was always a message inside. Saspi wished one of his tubes contained a sleeping potion, a strong one.

"No one thinks for themselves anymore," he continued. "Armenians born over here are too influenced by their women. Our son is eight years old now. You will have to teach him some discipline. It's always been lacking in your family's blood."

A long silence followed. Just as she thought he had fallen asleep he muttered, "Sex for a widow is unthinkable." With that Seto fell silent one final time and died.

Outside St. Mary's Armenian Apostolic Church teenagers are gathered around tables buying and selling CDs and cassettes of Armenian music. In the parking lot men are talking in the shade of the Chinese elm. She does not expect to find the Cubano here. He holds himself apart from others. Whenever he comes to the store he is quiet and alone. Saspi's friend Maria Theresa who lives in his building says she has never seen the Cubano bring anyone home to his apartment.

Saspi climbs the granite steps of the church and enters the sanctuary where her footsteps are muted by thick burgundy carpet. Slow, cheerless chords of the pipe organ mask whispers of the congregants. The stained glass windows are like illustrations from a children's Sunday school text, possessing none of the majesty of the cavernous stone cathedrals of Constantinople and Yerevan where her mother took her and Nahreen as children, where light fell to the stone floors from massive windows ignited by rosettes of cobalt, amethyst, and sun.

The church organist sits under the high scalloped ceiling with his back to the mass, pressing the yellowed keys, tapping the wooden foot pedals with his worn oxford shoes. The drone of the organ, a doleful underpinning to her older sister's voice in the choir, brings Saspi a winnowed calm. Nahreen's singing has always sounded like faded aristocracy, a zephyr blowing through heavy silks, the voice of a warrior, perfect in pitch and cadence. Electricity should be shut off when Nahreen sings.

An old woman stares at Saspi. Is it so obvious that she has come in search of a lover? What right has this old one to stare like this? If Saspi encounters the Cubano here, what will she say to this quiet man? She feels like an awkward girl, too dressed up for the occasion. She looks at her patent leather pumps and wonders how many women have broken an ankle looking for a man.

Saspi watches Father Magarian, hooded in velour and dark purple, drift past the altar rail. Does he feel something for the women in the congregation who seem to adore him? When he works in the rose garden behind St. Mary's, does he sweat like other men? Or is his smell always like that of the church, of bread and sugar, of dust and children? Unlike the younger priests, he does not trim his beard; it protrudes past his robe, somber and virile. She imagines the feel of it against her cheek and wonders how many of the other women think of him in this way. A younger priest sings the mass and swirls the incense burner back and forth on its brass chain, teasing the air with smoke.

Nahreen has told Saspi about the women who go to priests—unhappy wives of crippled soldiers, young girls just beginning to menstruate, widows, and whores. Behind heavy oak doors, the priests' chambers smell of sour wines and wells.

When she was seven years old, Saspi said to old Father Sarkissian, "Draw us the devil, Father." The priest led her to her mother in the quiet of an early mass. He lifted her mother's scarf, and whispered something. Saspi reached for her hand, but her mother pulled it away and closed her eyes in prayer.

For the first time in years, Saspi is comforted by burning the thin, white candle for her mother. She remembers dreaming of a house where she and her mother trailed their hands along walls and cornices of spice, and dipped their hands together into barrels of powdered nutmeg and rubbed it into each other's hair—to save their dreams, her mother said. Saspi misses her mother's hickory-colored hair, the lemony sweat on her skin. She misses her sense of order, the way she arranged the bottles and bags of seasonings by size and shape on the shelves and in the neatly papered cupboards.

When her mother spoke she pronounced her words slowly and with care as if a prelude to prayer. She dressed like a gypsy in a long purple skirt of regal wool showing the roundness of her hips, and in a yellow sleeveless blouse like a furious sun. She glowed against the hills. Saspi would clasp her mother's arms and stroke the warm skin, trying to cover it so men would not stare so often.

"Men always lie about their fathers," she told Saspi. "They invent battles they never fought. They'll tell you they rode with thousands of Balkan guerrilla fighters and harassed the Turks."

Saspi wonders if the Cubano was ever a hero. Had he defended their people? Had he ever killed? He was not yet born when Armenian blood of millions soaked into the sand at the feet of the Turks.

For years after her mother died Saspi rubbed nutmeg into her skin and hair at night. When she was a girl it protected her from her father and the harsh way he scrubbed her face with a mildewed woolen rag, against the emptiness of his prayers he whispered by her bed. He addressed God the way he did the accounting for the store, with no thought of perfection or grace, but with a petty tidiness like a forest animal that blindly washes its food in infected water but is satisfied that it is water nonetheless. Her father lived his life with a slate and a rag. Her mother languished in a dream of a house of nutmeg.

The mass has ended. Worshippers drift down a carpeted stairway toward the basement for the weekly Sunday brunch. Saspi doubts that the Cubano is here at all. She feels absurd in this place of immigrants' christenings and funerals.

Crumpled up in the mail slot of the store is a note from her friend Maria Theresa, an invitation for Saspi to come to her apartment tonight. She has invited the woman from the botanica, and promises that she will produce a revelation. Saspi would like that. Instead of trudging upstairs to her own apartment as she does every evening, tonight she will go to Maria Theresa's for a revelation.

She gathers a package of cracker bread, a can of Greek olives, a large piece of feta cheese, and a bag of pistachios. Saspi's husband disapproved of women who drank or smoked. To avoid fights and recriminations, Saspi simply didn't do either while he lived. But tonight she takes a bottle of Polish vodka from the liquor shelf and a pack of filtered cigarettes from behind the counter. It is a hot night and she carries no sweater.

Across the street, limousines and expensive automobiles are pulling up in front of Carmelita's. Bright yellow spotlights make the nightclub glamorous and alluring. She does not see the Cubano. Saspi walks past women dressed in silks, crepe, and chiffon billowing out from their young bodies. The perfumes remind her of nighttime crowds when she was a little girl, carnivals, the scent of jasmine and lilac, confections, and smoke. The glamour of the street disappears as she enters the Hollymount Apartment Hotel and climbs the ratty carpeted stairs. The place smells of lard and cooked peppers.

At the end of the hall, Maria Theresa stands in her doorway wearing slippers and a silk dressing gown embroidered in swans on a Chinese landscape. The apartment looks dark, as though she is not expecting anyone. From inside comes the smell of burning coffee and sage. The furnishings are a few brown plastic laminate tables with matching chairs, bulbous brass-colored lamps, and drab tufted love seats. Saspi empties the groceries onto the tiled kitchen counter.

"I've brought some things for your baby," she says.

Maria Theresa picks up the bottle of vodka and smiles at Saspi. "This is not for the baby."

A pounding comes from the apartment above. "All the time that *vieja* up there is making tortillas!" Maria Theresa shouts at the ceiling, "You're not in Zacatecas anymore, lady. Why don't you buy them at the Pioneer Market like everybody else?"

As Maria Theresa takes three glasses down from the cupboard, a tall, dark-skinned Hispanic woman emerges from the bedroom. She wears the white pants and jacket of a health practitioner. Her left eye appears to wander.

"Saspi, this is my friend, Reina." Maria Theresa places her hand respectfully on the woman's shoulder, guiding her close to Saspi. "Reina has a shop on Sunset, Saspi, *Olo*

Ochun Botanica. She gives advice."

Reina reminds Saspi of Romanian gypsies who passed through her village when she was a child. Her grandmother said that gypsies left severed hands underneath childrens' beds and warned that she should never look down there or the lonely hands would leap up and throttle her.

As Reina moves she makes the apartment walls darken. She clasps Saspi's hand and speaks in a deep alto voice, "Your friend Maria Theresa is concerned for you. She says you are fixing to love someone and need help with that." Reina does not move her eyes. One seems to look deep into Saspi, and the other stares somewhere else.

Maria Theresa fills the glasses with vodka, and the three women drink. *"Que sabrosa, que rica,* Saspi. My boyfriends never drink anything this good." Maria Theresa scrunches up her face and shudders as the liquor flows down her throat.

She sniffs the perfume on Saspi's wrist and smiles. "It's time for the Cubano, Saspi. Are you in love with him?"

Saspi feels her face turn warm.

Maria Theresa giggles, "He's as handsome as any TV game-show host, Saspi. He looks like Cantinflas, the movie star."

Saspi leans forward in her chair. "He dresses like a dance instructor. And his mustache looks as if it's made of enamel paint."

"When you are close to him, what happens?" Maria Theresa's face is flushed and beautiful.

To Saspi this is a wonderful new game. "When he comes in the store I want to pull his stubby little ears."

"Take him, Saspi, make him your sweetheart."

"Before he keels over and dies, eh?"

Reina startles Saspi as she suddenly leans forward and puts a match to a small twist of verbena. It is the hour of revelation. She extinguishes the flame with her fingers, letting the fragrant herb smolder in the ashtray. Reina has brought her skills and tangents in a floral cloth bag. She centers a translucent human-shaped candle on the glass coffee table and rings it with small envelopes of powders and a dozen postcards—images of God, saints, Jesus Christ, visions of purgatory and hell. A clear cellophane bag contains a tiny horseshoe magnet, iron filings, sequins, a seed pod, and a drawing of an Aztec soldier atop a horse with the Virgin of Guadalupe perched upon the horn of his saddle. There is a card with photographs of women in bathing suits and sheer peignoirs. Reina places this card in front of Saspi.

She slices open an envelope labeled *Polvo Especial* and taps out into a saucer a powder like a drug the color of talc. "This is *Ven a Mi*." Reina speaks slowly and without expression. "It will give you good results in love between a man and a woman. Rub it on your neck and chest after you bathe. It calls love to you."

Reina draws her fingertips across the cards as if prompting thoughts or chemistry. She raises the candle up toward the ceiling light. A second, thinner body appears within it, an echo of rose. "When you are drawing a lover closer, you must make a mixture of sugar and honey and pour it over the top of the candle so it dribbles down the sides. A sweetness of love will attract him to you. Put your name four times down the center, at either side of it, and around the head. You burn it three times a day and pray. It represents humankind."

Saspi stares at the candle. The shape of breasts and a penis have appeared upon it. Reina fingers a card of a female figure clothed in pink. "This is la Virgin de la Carridad. You know Santaria? People pray to la Virgin in Cuba. They like her in Cuba. Goddess of Compassion."

"Where do you come from?" asks Saspi.

"I am from the old Managua before it was destroyed in the Christmas Eve earthquake and will never be again."

Reina stares fixedly at Saspi and begins running her hands very quickly over the table, pausing momentarily to point out details in the cards. "My ladies here," she says tapping the cards, "they possess things."

Saspi sees the image of a white jackass grazing in moss, a toad partly obscured by granite, a white owl perched in the crotch of a hill, a dog held aloft by bat wings, its face a Chinese war mask. Eve has loosed the apple. Bosomless nymphs bury their faces in her hair. They are rose dust. A serpent yearns to be her garment. Its jaw grazes her breast.

"My ladies ride serpents like they are lawn toys," Reina declares. "Nobody lies to them."

An etched figure in a high-waisted, caramel-colored gown attends the long chalky corpse of an old woman laid out on a bier of stone and touches her arm. The walls are blood and velvet. A figure is bent over a garden of lilies of the valley. She counts the blossoms among the folds of her dress.

Reina places two more cards in front of Saspi—a photograph of two lovers holding flowers and regarding each other from windows in separate houses, and a drawing of a man and woman chained together by the sea. "They are husband and wife. She is his tormentor. Her lover is splayed out on a rock nearby. His arms hide his face."

Saspi picks up the card. "My husband is dead twenty years and probably still feels tormented."

"The lover in the card is your Cubano," Maria Theresa says, glancing out the window. "He is on duty tonight, look quickly."

On the sidewalk below, the tiny figure of the Cubano ushers people briskly to and fro, helping women on with their wraps, offering his arm, opening car doors.

Maria Theresa pulls Saspi toward the window. "He's walking across the street. He's heading for your place."

The Cubano saunters casually across the broad avenue and peers into the black windows of Saspi's store and tries the locked gate.

Maria Theresa clutches Saspi's hand. "He's come for you, Saspi."

"He's just looking for cigarettes." Saspi's voice sounds tremulous and hesitant.

"No, no. It is working, honey. He's like the little remote-controlled race car I gave my nephew. Just move the joy-stick and it goes where you want it to."

Across the street the store is shuttered and dark. The Cubano appears to be waiting quietly by Saspi's door. He doesn't lean against the flagstone facade or light a cigarette. He simply stands there, attentive, alert, waiting.

He is the picture of Saspi's desires.

"Go," Maria Theresa says urgently.

Saspi walks to the door. "I'm going to meet him." She is surprised at her own words. She wonders if this is another faithless gesture. She watches Reina gather up her cards, gently laying one atop the other. She imagines placing vestments upon Reina's shoulders, long floral gowns, resplendent and rich. Reina, queen of cards and powders, expounder of the saints.

Saspi opens the apartment door. For a moment she studies Maria Theresa, the Mayan curve to her cheek, the stories in her eyes, dark as alleys. Saspi wonders if she has been lied to all her life. Maybe everyone lives like this.

She crosses the street toward the store, blinded for a moment by the spotlights at Carmelita's. She stares into the violet shadows and feels a warm Santa Ana wind on her face. The sky is a fine net of gauze streaked with black. The trees are healthy and thick with wide yellow blossoms, the yellow of old country weddings. This is a night free of memory.

She Stands in the Cold Water
James Lowell McPherson

She stands in the cold water, facing
south toward an invisible island.
In the Sunday morning quiet
the redwing blackbirds
shuffle nervously in a thicket
behind the beach. The loon
makes no sound at all in its
purposeful passage.

For sixty years and more
she has tested the waters
this way. Soon she will take
the plunge. Intrepid swimmer.
For her there is never
backing out. Never. She will dive
into the salt waves and there will be
friendliness and fellowship and
sisterhood, and a spot of
solitude.

Her landlocked husband, a creature of air
and dirt, leans against a boulder
and watches her. His silence
goes with her, and with the loon.
He guards towel, glasses, sandals.
His heart flutters in the thicket.

He rests quietly at the margin
of the liquid world, waiting.
When she rises, rebaptized,
from the sea, she will find
a harbor here.

Then and Now
Phyllis King

In the beginning
he was light in my arms.
Even in the act of love
I was afraid he would float away.
Only the sharp brush of our pubic bones
made me sure he would stay.
Now heavier with age
we sink into each other.
Comfort of flesh and warm clasp
assure us of permanence.

Sometimes I think
he hates the balding head,
the Santa Claus beard,
the comfortable waist,
that mask the fragile
and elusive spirit
that still floats
lightly in my arms.

photo by Katie Utter

For an Anniversary
Gailmarie Pahmeier

"...still willingly I rage with you..."
  —A. Wilbur Stevens

Love, if I leave our life before you,
take this, my kitchen, as legacy.
Take the cayenne, the andouille,
the boudin, the hard, hard bread.
Serve fresh vegetables steamed
with vinegar, peppers to suck
from their stems, orange spice tea.
Make sure there is ice, chicory coffee.
Give everyone, including children, cloth napkins.
After dinner there should be music,
roll up the rugs and dance.

Love, if I leave our life before you,
imagine me in the arms of a boy
whose pickup truck carries his dreams.
I'll be eating apples, leaving lipstick on cans,
listening to rain-delayed games on the radio.
Love, whatever passes, I promise—
in our old age we will not want.
Here, come here. Taste this.

What Remains
Amy L. Uyematsu

Older now, the woman is
guarding the passageway—
after children have left
her room, she dances
watches herself move
hips and hair
to this slow saxophoned phrase

retracing the steps
only lighter now, the blue
curl of melodies she
can finally call her own—
keeping time
to the noiseless
breath, keeping time
to the jazzman.

The Widow and the Gigolo
Marion Zola

Here we sit dearest, both of us mad,
my love is dead and you're holding my hand.
Who would guess from that devoted gaze—
who but I , the willing victim, knows
the studied artifice that keeps it there?
It's all right, you know, to pose this way for
one another: the young but jaded seeker
after deeper, fuller wines who, in spite
of the arrangement, finds her quite delightful.
I, the mundane widow who, forsaking
pride for pleasure, believes his tenderness.

Last night, when I'd drunk too much and ordered
the band to play on, you echoed my shouts
as if it were the thing to do—clever you.
How long could it have taken to acquire
the art of petty conversation? Speaking
of food and who is here and what is chic
bores me dear. But never mind. Later when
it's dark and those wretched bells keep ringing
I won't cross the Piazza de San Marco alone,
and you, without a better place to go,
may accompany me home.

A Woman Like That
Peter Meinke

His legs throbbed every morning when he got up and stumbled to the bathroom. Rotten to get old, he thought. No good'll come of it. He looked in the mirror at his grizzled face. It's also rotten to be young, he remembered, and tried to think of when he had been happiest. My damn nose is growing longer! Could that be possible?

Daniel Daniels was sixty-eight and had been a moderately successful man, much loved by everyone, as moderately successful people tend to be. For forty years he ran a prosperous florist's shop in Bridgeport, before selling the business two years ago and joining the retirees in St. Petersburg. He had hoped the sea air would take the pains out of his hands and legs.

He was probably happiest in his thirties. He had loved his wife, his two good kids and, briefly, a mistress—Nancy Miller—who was his best friend. There was never talk of divorce, so their affair, though secret, had been a pleasant and companionable exception to the terror and guilt that usually accompany such activities. In fact, the four of them got along perfectly until the Millers moved away. And that had been that. The only real trouble with Daniel's wife, Linda, was her high-pitched voice, which grated on his nerves more and more as the years wore on.

There must have been other troubles, too, but at this

point, ten years after her death, Daniel couldn't remember what they were; he remembered instead how pretty she was, how she would skip like a six-year-old when she was happy, how one martini would make her giggly and coquettish.

He had been lonely after she died, and his move to St. Petersburg had been taken partially to throw off this loneliness. He could have stayed with his children, who were married and well enough off, but they had their own concerns and he sensed he wasn't one of their major ones.

Now, for the first time in years, Daniel felt some of that old excitement coming back, and he shaved with care. He was going fishing with Julia Dodson! At least his hands were still steady, not like some of those poor old duffers he'd met sitting on the benches downtown where he went every day for his exercise. He'd walk up and down the pier, sometimes feeding the waddling pelicans, and then he'd play shuffleboard at the Mirror Lake Park in the afternoon.

That was where he had met Julia. Daniel, tall and lean, was naturally coordinated, a notable first baseman with the Bridgeport Bombers (forty years ago! Who the hell was president then?) and, within a month of his arrival in St. Petersburg, had become a respected shuffleboard player. Julia Dodson was one of the regular group of people who came to watch the men play.

Julia was from New Haven; they'd practically been neighbors! She had lived in St. Petersburg for three years, but her heart remained up North. Although she was sixty-two (she said), she looked younger. Her hair was white, piled on top of her head when it was hot, but her skin was still young—energy bloomed through her face and exploded out of her dark eyes. She was small and trim and always managed to look cool, especially among the overweight, red-faced, perspiring dowagers who frequented the park.

Widowed for eight years, Julia had been unable, on her small pension, to keep her lovely house in New Haven, and had come to St. Petersburg because of the gentler climate, which indeed she enjoyed. But the humid summers, the increasing numbers of tourists, and her tiny furnished flat oppressed her.

It wasn't long before Daniel saw her apartment, little more than an efficiency, some distance from the water, but not all that far from Daniel's more spacious quarters in a dignified old hotel. To his surprise, it was tasteless and common. Julia dressed stylishly in a muted, understated way, but her flat was loud, almost garish. The pictures and ornaments could have been won at a country fair, and she served him a cordon bleu meal on green plastic plates.

"You see why I hate it so," she said. "I've always been a house person. This is what the place was like when I found it, and I can't really bring myself to do anything with it; anything decent is so expensive. I'm in here as little as possible."

After that, they always met at his place. They spent long evenings together; sometimes they went out dancing at the casino in Gulfport. They enjoyed that, but it was vaguely depressing, too—just the old folks, doing the old dances: the waltz, the fox-trot, the tango. It seemed unnatural somehow, like premature burial. The young people were elsewhere, at the disco maybe, or the roller rink.

During the day she would walk around the lake with

him, and watch him at his afternoon shuffleboard game. They went fishing a few times off the pier, and he would gallantly bait her hook and unhook the fish, usually flipping it to a pelican. They could see the fish jumping in its gullet—now that's premature burial, he thought. One day she caught a large striped sheepshead; he cleaned and filleted it, and she cooked it ceremoniously in his kitchen—candlelight and white wine, brandy and coffee.

Daniel had never been a particularly sensual man, but he was still virile and the lovely young girls walking along the pier would sometimes surprise him by bringing tears to his eyes. Why tears, idiot? Because the girls were no longer for him, he supposed; because they never even saw him. And because they would get old, too, sooner than they thought.

Prostitutes sometimes hung around outside the bars near the pier, but Daniel was afraid to approach them. Suppose they were diseased, suppose he accosted a plain-clothes policewoman? He fantasized the headlines: "Old Geezer Arrested." "Disgusting Display by Senior Citizen." "Seamy Seaside Sex." So he had remained celibate.

But on this evening of the candlelit dinner—he had shaved so carefully!—Julia had stayed overnight. She seemed a little tipsy, and maybe he was, too. They had danced to radio music, and he kissed her. They were standing by the open bedroom door. She looked at him a long time, smiling.

"Daniel Daniels," she said. "What a funny funny name name." She smiled some more. "After all," she said, "we're not children."

The next morning, looking at her, he thought his heart would crack open. She looked so fragile, so small and vulnerable. How lucky he was, at his age! But when she awoke, he only joked.

"This is obscene," he told her. "I'm sixty-eight years old. I'm liable to have a heart attack."

Julia laughed. "'Grow old along with me, the best is yet to be." She leaned back on the pillow and rolled her eyes. "And besides, old goats like you don't have heart attacks."

"What happens to us?"

"Old goats like you disappear into the woods or mountains and are never seen again, except from a distance, where you seem to be dancing or doing something illegal with some creature or other."

"I think I'll do something illegal with you right now."

"Oh, I hope so!"

So their affair had begun. They were just like kids; for six months they had been inseparable. They had discussed marriage, they discussed "living in sin." Daniel asked her to move in with him, but she wouldn't. She had an *idée fixe:* she wanted to live in a real house again, like real people.

He was uneasy with this idea, but in some ways the timing was right. Her flat was unsuitable, certainly, and his hotel had fallen on difficult times. There were strong rumors that it was going to be remodeled into an office building, and Daniel and the other residents would have to move—a very discouraging prospect.

But to take on a house! It wasn't the money—Daniel was by no means tightfisted, though this would severely deplete his savings; rather it was the work involved. He didn't want to maintain a house, put washers in leaky taps, clean out the gutters, mow the lawn. Hotel living was easy—all those little jobs are done for you.

Julia, however, had made up her mind, and her enthusiasm was catching. "Just the two of us, with our own property again! A garden and privacy, and a place to be proud of."

She took the lead, and followed the ads, and contacted the owners and real estate agents. They looked at dozens of places, but nothing appealed to her.

One day she came to his room, shining with excitement. "I've seen the perfect house," she said. "The owners are away but the real estate woman has given me the key. We can go and see it this morning."

They drove there in Daniel's car. Julia had no car; in fact, she seemed to have almost no worldly goods whatsoever.

And the house *was* lovely. It stood in a winding, tree-lined street on the outskirts of town. There were azaleas and camellias and jasmine in the front garden, which was cottage-scale and manageable, instead of the usual sprawling lawn. Inside, Daniel could see why it appealed to her. It was furnished with rocking-chairs, deep soft sofas, old desks, bookshelves; exactly what he knew she wanted. He had to admit that the house was just like her, right down to the furnishings.

But there were many drawbacks. It was in bad condition and needed a lot of work. It was more than he wanted to spend. It was a long way from the nearest supermarket, and the public transportation was unreliable—which was all right with Daniel, because he had a car and enjoyed a morning jaunt to the shops. But how could Julia get around? They'd need another car.

None of this disturbed Julia. "It's perfect for us!" And she swept him up with her until he agreed: It *would* be wonderful. He made an offer on Wednesday, the sale being somewhat complicated by the absentee owner, named Haworth, but before too many days passed all the papers were signed, all the checks handed over (with a faster beating heart), and the keys given to Daniel.

Julia had stayed away, perhaps out of delicacy, from these financial transactions. And she had so much to do: some shopping, some packing, final arrangements with her apartment. Daniel was to pick her up the next day; they would begin moving in, and then next week (or next month—whenever they felt truly ready) they would be married.

He couldn't sleep all night: he was already feeling like a newlywed. He noticed his aches and pains had seemed to gradually disappear since he had known her. He got up early and bought a huge bouquet of white chrysanthemums (her favorite) from one of the corner flower girls— giving the puzzled teenager a five-dollar tip and a moony grin—and walked to Julia's apartment complex. Her place was on the third floor. He hiked up and rang the bell.

There was no answer. She always was a late sleeper, but today was a special day; Daniel found himself a little irritated. Then he thought, "This is the first time I've felt irritated in six months. Not bad. I used to live with irritation, an oyster with his pearl."

He strolled down to the pier, the chrysanthemums held

high in his hand like an Olympic torch of love, and smiled idiotically at everyone who came by.

At lunch time he went back again, but she still didn't answer. This is getting ridiculous, he thought. He walked over to the Sandpiper, where they often met for lunch, then drove out to the house. *Their house.* He went in and opened some of the windows; they were casement windows and not all of them worked. He phoned her apartment: nothing. Daniel was beginning to worry. He didn't like surprises.

Finally, he drove back to her apartment and waited. When she hadn't returned by six o'clock, he went downstairs to the caretaker's room, but he was also out. In desperation, Daniel climbed back upstairs and knocked on the door of the apartment next to Julia's. A plump, middle-aged woman opened the door.

"I'm sorry to trouble you, but I'm looking for Mrs. Dodson."

"You must have the wrong apartment. I'm Mary Buxton." She fluttered curling false eyelashes at him.

"Yes, of course," said Daniel. "What I mean is, I thought you might have seen her today."

"I don't know any Mrs. Dodson." She put her hand on the doorknob.

"She lives next door. I thought perhaps you'd know her."

"Oh, no, Sally Williams lives there, but she isn't there either. She's away a lot." Flutter, flutter. Daniel resisted an urge to shake the curlers out of her hair.

"Julia Dodson. She's a small lady with long, white hair, usually done up like this." He made vague gestures over his head, forgetting he was still clutching the chrysanthemums.

Mary Buxton smiled. "Oh, you must mean Julie Haworth. She stays here sometimes when Sally is away. Keeps an eye on things, you know. I've had coffee with her and Sally."

"Haworth?" He remembered the name. "Julia Dodson doesn't live here?" His brain was beginning to spin.

"No, Julie *Haworth*—it must be the same person, a very pretty little lady, she lives in a house somewhere but she hates it. All she wants to do is move to New England somewhere, but nobody will buy her house and she has no money. She really hates St. Petersburg. I don't know why she came in the first place. I like it here, myself, even though..."

Daniel's voice was shaking. "Do you know where she lives?"

"No. Somewhere on the edge of town, out in the boonies. Lots of trees, she said. Have you seen it? Why did you think her name was Dodson?"

But Daniel had already turned away. He ran outside, limped down the street, and turned blindly toward the pier, sitting down on one of the benches there, still holding the chrysanthemums.

After a while, tears ran down his face, but he was surprised to find that he was smiling, too. Dammit! She sold me her own goddamn house! What a woman!

Various plans whirled through his head: Go after her, bring her back; go to the police; go after her, wring her sweet neck. Put the house on the market, burn it down. Keep it as a souvenir. A young girl jogged by, her feet hardly touching the ground.

He had been a fool, certainly. Still, his heart went out to her. He understood her perfectly. Someone had said the hardest thing to understand about life is that we can understand it so well. The audacity of it! The bravery! If he ever found another woman, which was unlikely, Daniel wanted a woman like that.

He sat there as evening rolled in over the bay, the bright sailboats fading in the dark. Pelicans edged toward him, looking for handouts. He tossed the chrysanthemums over the railing. In the black water they began floating away from the pier, like sea anemones heading home.

Papier-Mache
Mary Elizabeth Parker

Ellen rose awkwardly from kneeling before her bedroom chest and caught a glimpse of herself in the closet mirror: She looked like a ship's survivor grabbing at flotsam. Her face was smudged, her hair was unpinned. A flimsy carton of six harmonicas, district issue from 1963, was clutched in one hand, and clutched in the other was a Christmas apron handsewn for her by someone's mother.

An Amy's mother, she thought she remembered. The apron was pristine, still folded in tissue paper. She tied it around her waist. The white organza scratched and pricked her nose with must. She ran her palm down the appliquéd holly on the pocket, honoring Amy's mother's gift thirty years too late.

But she had to work steadily and try not to think, just move methodically from chest to bureau to closet to clean everything out. Jill would be here soon to start removing furniture, and Jill wanted anything else gone.

"Just keep the essentials, stuff you can't live without," she had said, and Ellen wondered if her daughter had any idea what that meant. Jill herself owned a nearly bare apartment, a motorcycle, a closetful of purple shifts, and a daughter, Augusta, three, as black-haired and sturdy as herself. Jill would make short work of this room, six trash bags and done, Ellen knew. Which was why she had refused to let Jill help.

Her own hands were moving more and more slowly in their task, as recesses of closets and drawers continued to yield shy loot: scribbled drawings and crayoned Valentine's cards, penciled scores of holiday songs she'd written for students to sing. She pored through the pile and found her favorite. "I wish I were one of Columbus's men, sailing over the blue," she sang tinnily to the room, "I wish those days could come back again, sailing over the blue." It sounded thin with no child's voice joining in. She'd teach it to Augusta, then, when they were all living in Jill's house; there had to be some way to fit in there.

Snow was still trailing down outside, and she scooted herself over to the window to rest her forehead for a moment against the icy panes. She wiped her perspiring face with the fancy apron.

There was so much here, it seemed as if she had kept everything: broken pairs of scissors, nubs of chalk, a district commendation from 1978, warnings not to requisition too much paste, stacks of spelling papers, stubby black pencils. She sat squarely in the middle and ran her hands over all this sea of objects, as if to raise from them some kind of Braille, a meaning. Finally, she took one harmonica from the package of six, for Augusta, and raised her hand over the trash bag to dump the rest.

Then she stopped for a moment. She didn't want to pare down further. She'd felt just fine living with all these objects, like acorns tucked into the niches of her apartment, still fat with possibility. Even though Arthur had been gone five years, she had not been too lonely, with her teaching. And although his hospital bills had eaten a large chunk of savings, she had managed all right since retiring last year.

But mother and daughter living together, she would never have dreamed that in her worst nightmares. Still, there was no help for it: Her certificates of deposit were failing as interest rates dropped further, and Jill had no money either—just too much expensive space after the divorce. Ex-husband, Tory, career army, was posted in a desert somewhere. She, Ellen, was being shunted in to take his place.

Ellen groaned at the thought of the bedroom in Jill's apartment, the ceiling—that had once been a modest white—sloppily painted with stars like a captured cosmos. Where on those electric-blue walls could her lace samplers make any kind of statement? How could she drape her cream-and-melon afghan over Jill's leather couch which was smudged with fingerprints? She imagined her bath set, blue cabbage roses on white, grimed by Augusta's hands in Jill's red bathroom with its gunmetal tub.

Then, in a shoe box stuffed with milk money receipts, Ellen found the directions for making a pig. Like the papier-mache pig which had stood on her desk for twenty-three years, with her name looped around it in lavender script: Mrs. Lyles. Students had shanghaied it often, tucking it under their skinny arms and hauling it around the room, then perching it on top of the history corner, so that George Washington wore a pig on his head.

Ellen sat back on her haunches, forgetting that this was not a position she could rise from gracefully anymore. She reached for the phone on the bedside table and called Jill.

"I hope you're ready," Jill said, before Ellen could even get a word out. "I've got the van from Gerry, but I have to bring it back tonight. It's not going to be easy hauling stuff through this snow."

There was a random, scraping background noise as Jill spoke, and Ellen could see her daughter knifing crumbs out from a crack in the tabletop, or using a matchstick to poke mud from her boot soles. She had never in Jill's life seen her sit still.

"I'll help you move as much as I can when you get here," Ellen said, "but it's got to be later. There's something I forgot to do. Give me two hours," she said, and hung up.

Dipping and laving until the strips came out shining, she prepared newspaper strips in a bowl of thin paste. It was a dreaming motion, as smooth and deliberate as the snow arcing past the kitchen window. Then, aware of each dip of her too-pale, fleshy wrists, she laid the strips the length of the kitchen table. She had already fashioned a wire frame, with scraps gleaned from the utility cupboard.

Now, she held the wire head lightly and laid the first strips of papier-mache over it. It had been a long time since she'd worked like this. The menagerie of animals she'd formed for her first students—lamb, ostrich, alligator, pig—were all probably smashed to powder somewhere. As she built up this new pig's head, eye sockets and jowls and protrusion for a snout, her hands remembered the first pig she had designed years ago.

It had been feminine, round, painted pale pink and then

etched with blue violets. She'd had a rough job to keep one of the boys from squeezing it, loving it too hard, when it was brought into class. Jill was like that boy, almost. Even now as an adult, Jill had clumsy boy's hands. Hands that checked the riggings for new bungee jumpers, then her own rigging before she flung herself out on the sky. What if Jill died that way, a demonstration leap, and she, Ellen, was the one left to raise Augusta? But she didn't want to think of that now. Make this pig, she told herself, just do it. She was building up the fat body now, the old rhythm fully alert in her hands.

She wrapped the last gummy strip around the belly of the pig. The pig was pale and wet, still newsprint black-and-white. Ellen's palms rested lightly on the pig head, as if it were a child's skull. Then she heard Jill drive up below, the tires of the van backing and scraping.

Jill burst into the kitchen and Ellen watched her appraise the piles of things still unsorted, unpacked. "I can't believe it, Elly," Jill said. "What is this? You were supposed to get this stuff out of here."

Ellen didn't answer. Although she was by now used to the familiar "Elly," it was still not the way she thought a mother should be addressed.

Without glancing at the pig, Jill marched through the still-cluttered apartment, her high-heeled boots pocking the floor with icy mud, a pacifier bobbing in her mouth. Jill was trying to quit smoking, and pacifiers were stylish, very de rigueur in California, she had said.

Augusta came behind Jill, swaggering too, even though her small, fat legs were still encased in snow pants.

Copying her mother, Augusta stuffed paper scraps into trash bags. Then she swung around to Ellen for approval, her eyes shining. Her hands grabbed at a knickknack shelf for support and a cut-glass dragonfly slid off the shelf and broke. Shy now, Augusta brought the dragonfly to Ellen, poking the leg into the broken-off place to try to make it fit.

Then Augusta's eye was caught by the pig. She climbed onto a kitchen chair and wrapped her arms around the pig. "I like it, Grandma Elly," she said. "It can be my puppy."

Ellen felt another presence at her side. Jill was standing there, no longer stomping around and stuffing things in boxes. "That's not a puppy, Gussie, hon," Jill said. "That's a Violetta Pig. Pretty soon, it'll have violets all over—little blue flowers." Jill was wearing a half-smile that worked oddly around the pacifier in her mouth.

Ellen stared. Yes, she had named the pig Violetta. But how had Jill remembered that? Even at that age, Jill was too busy falling out of trees, being the boy that Arthur never had. Now Jill was chucking this pig under the chin, as if the pig could enjoy it. She said, "If you'd made me one of these when I was a kid, I wouldn't have ruined it, you know. I tried to make a cat once on my own, but I couldn't get the tail to stay on." Ellen tried to imagine Jill's hands shaping a fragile length of wire. She looked at her large, forceful daughter, and at Augusta, who would probably be as forceful. Then she gently moved Augusta's thumb, which was pressing down against the pig's still-not-cemented ear, and looked around the kitchen for a clean cloth to drape the pig. There were three remaining boxes to be filled, and the pig could balance in one. It was still snowing, but if they went down the steps carefully, maybe nothing would break.

photo by Teresa Tamura

Spring Cleaning
Sharon H. Nelson

The skeletons we keep in the closet
come out from time to time to clank their bones.
These are the ghosts we've settled with,
reminders of old wounds, lessons learned, tucked away,
out of sight, out of mind.

We push them back amongst the jumble,
try to keep them pressed down under
the out-of-season blankets,
equipment of sports we no longer practice,
the pile of too-good-for-the-rag-bag clothes we thought
we'd wash and iron and take along
to the church bazaar or crisis centre.
But we seldom get to it, to that final job
of tidying the bottom of the bottommost cupboard.

Some of us are organized, efficient.
The skates and football helmets our children outgrew
were traded in or up or out years ago.
We are frugal; *waste not, want not.*

Our minds are full of these old adages
we learned to keep in store,
along with strange, no longer useful bits:

great-grandmother's tissue-wrapped muff,
granny's rusting fruitcake tins,
annually inspected and ruefully rewrapped,
repacked, replaced, a set of things
our childhood fancies linger in.

Past and future coalesce
in objects worn but not worn out,
the lines and things we learned to keep,
in the keeping of which we learned to acquiesce.

Perhaps it's wool, or bolts of cloth, or the family silver.
There's always something in there,
something with some weight to it,
something at the backs of cupboards,
to hold down the visions we cannot afford to see,
that we overlook most purposefully.

We are creatures intent on survival,
single-minded, focused. Our mothers told us:
what you don't know can't hurt you.
Our mothers were liars, liars all.

They had cupboards too, and never told
what they kept there. Instead, exemplary, they taught
good housekeeping; amidst the neat and clean, they allowed
that every woman needs her special drawer
for hat pins, bits of string, and souvenirs
and a single cupboard for long-term storage,
a place to hide what won't fit in.

At the backs of our mothers'
messiest cupboards
our lives begin.

Harvest
Shirley Vogler Meister

With gusto, she plunged her hands
into pumpkin pulp, pulling
and scooping until the innards
and seeds slipped loose, and juice
ran down her arms in yellow trickles:
she didn't know she was purging pain.

Watching his wife, he finally felt
the scraping and cutting—the wounds
of the flesh—as if they were his own;
three decades of floods and droughts
on the grounds of marriage come
to harvest in a Hoosier heart
distracted by family pressures.

Newly-made bread and apple butter,
hay barns warmed by cattle breath,
farmwork under a waning sun,
tall purple phlox fading into fall,
pumpkin pies cooling on Halloween—
keen sensations blend into panic
and urgency, like the need to secure
the livestock before a blizzard hits.

Too late, too *tired*. Emotions sleep
like fallow fields, yearning for new
springs, new dreams: winter follows
autumn, and the pungent pumpkin
is frozen in plastic, waiting.

Spring without Burpee Seeds
Jean Blackmon

Every spring I take stock.

I look around my village to see what we might have lost since this time last year. The feed store still sells baby chicks. Someone plowed the fields at the north end again, and buds are swelling on the apple trees.

At my store, the Frontier Mart, we still sell asparagus gathered from along the irrigation ditch, and children still buy jacks, jump ropes, and kites. But near the door between the Popsicle freezer and the fifty-pound dog food, the garden seeds are gone.

Last year I received a letter from Mr. Burpee saying we hadn't sold enough to warrant his sending more. I miss getting the big parcel where tab A slid into slot B, and all that cardboard folded magically into a display of snap-dragons and four-o'clocks, zucchini, carrots, and lima beans.

No sooner would I assemble the display than old men in coveralls would come to read the seed packets, to talk about sunlight, soil, and water requirements, to count the days until maturity. They fingered the envelopes like kids at the candy counter, then carried their selections away like packets of promise.

Three of my seed customers were Ramon and Julio Tenorio and Walter Ackerson. Maybe a storekeeper shouldn't play favorites, but in nineteen years of business, Ramon, Julio, and Walter are at the top of my list.

They grew corn and cabbage and raised pigs. Ramon and Julio were brothers from one of the old families. On spring mornings Julio and his horse, Smokey, plowed the field at the corner of Tenorio and Corrales Roads. Walter was a cowboy who had come down from Colorado in the 1940s. He's the only eighty-two-year-old I've known who rode his horse every day.

Ramon and Walter were best friends who traveled together. When Walter's car wouldn't start, they rode to my store on a tractor with Ramon in the driver's seat and Walter standing alongside. They bought Jimmy Dean sausage, single-edge razor blades, and shaving cream in a cup with a bristle brush. Heading home, the old tractor crept along the two-lane road at fifteen miles per hour, and cars moved into the left lane to pass. Traffic was light then, tractors commonplace.

On Friday nights when I saw Ramon and Walter's tractor parked at the Territorial House, I'd stop and find them in the bar. Ramon talked about family and farming; Walter told about his days as a cowboy on the Black Ranch. Around eleven I'd say, "Time for me to go. You guys behave."

Ramon looked offended. "I *always* behave," he said. "I work hard and when I go to church, I keep my eyes off the young girls."

Walter snorted and mumbled something about blowing smoke.

Julio, Ramon, and Walter haven't been in the store for a

long time now. We didn't mark their last visit or say good-bye. One day we just realized they hadn't come in.

I'm told Julio and Ramon died more than a year ago, and Walter's gone now, too. I think of them whenever I think of spring and farming and Burpee seeds. It makes me look around to see what is missing. Then I memorize what we have left in case it turns up missing next year. What I'm trying to say is, if I'd known it was my last Burpee seed display, I would have paid more attention.

photo by Eliud Martinez

Sam, At Sixty
Pat Schneider

He opens the front door with the force of a minor hurricane, the great bulk of him led by his belly, which is held in only metaphorically by wide, red suspenders. His face is bushy with beard; he feels like a warm version of the north wind, all blow, hair going white, beard wild with curl. His cap is blue with a protruding bill and white letters proclaiming, Friends Don't Let Friends Drive Fords.

"Hell-*o*?" he yells, the last syllable lifting, a question. Under the red suspenders, an orange tomcat grimaces on his T-shirt above the words, Gimme Coffee, Nobody Gets Hurt.

He brings what I have lost: Ozark country humor, sausage and milk gravy, biscuits, cornbread, lightning bugs at dusk, a million grasshoppers at noon.

He has left his truck's motor running, parked as far onto my lawn as the oak tree will allow. "Had a delivery in North Adams," he says, planting a wet, mustached kiss on my mouth. "Got any coffee?"

It's a busy day. I have plans. But I would make a pot of coffee for my brother if the world were coming to an end. Because the world we knew together is coming to an end, and he's the only one who remembers the day I roller-skated too fast down the hill, how I fell—how he picked me up and called me by my childhood name.

The Gathering
Lois Tschetter Hjelmstad

We sit around a table
in an unfamiliar restaurant—
my brother, my sister, and I
our mates smiling at us
from across the table
our parents (who are eighty-six)
completing the circle

The tinkle of ice in other glasses
the murmur of other conversations
are background to our communion

It has taken a long time
to come to this place
    past the early rivalry
    past the fierce competition
    past the wary friendliness
    past the hurts, both small and large

But somehow
we finally
cut to the chase

We lucked out—
it wasn't too late

I revel in the peaceful knowledge
I sigh for the lost years
I weep for the short tomorrow

Investing
Savina Roxas

I sit, pencil in hand, sorting out different publications on investing for good future returns. Under current holdings in my file, I'll put, "The Mathematics of Investing," and under technical analysis, "Baron's Financial Table."

Regulations, handbooks, and directories I'll put on the bookshelf. The next publication, "How to Draw Up Your Own Will," I won't file or put on the shelf. Better look at it right away. Need a well-documented will for the end of the best-is-yet-to-come years. Don't want the children to have any hassles about it when I'm gone.

If I call Swanson & Phillips, Esq. to draw up the will, it will cost $150 an hour, even just to talk on the phone. I'll take a stab at it myself. I'm sure that's why my brother-in-law is sending me all this stuff. Wants me to be a self-sufficient widow.

Actually, my sole beneficiary should be St. Anthony's Church. Hardly ever see the children. Too busy with their own lives, I suppose. Nothing I say or do brings them around very often.

Since Ed died two years ago, my life revolves around the church: Monday, Christian Women's Club; Tuesday, Bible Study; Wednesday, Tutor a Child in the School Program; Friday, Bridge Club; Saturday, Bingo; and of course, Mass on Sunday.

Then Ed's brother, in addition to all the other financial publications, gave me a subscription to the *Wall Street Journal*. He said, "This'll keep you out of the mischief of buying high and selling low." No doubt, referring to the Pittsburgh Brewing stock I bought at ten and unloaded at fifty cents on the dollar.

It takes great diplomacy to keep from letting him know that I just can't face the daily rundown of facts and figures on investing that appears in the *Journal*. So I'm giving it to my next-door neighbor, Bill, who has time and an interest in that sort of thing. All I ask of him is that he keep me updated on certain stock information to keep me solvent.

That's how I came to develop some interest in my aloof neighbors. In all the years they've lived next door, we've done no more than wave to each other. Lately, I've noticed that Elsie is turning into a grim-faced old lady. Hardly even waves now.

When Bill retired, I thought this might make a difference, make him and his wife friendlier. It didn't. Never see their children or friends coming and going from their house any more. But I do see Elsie going and coming from her daily walk. Often wish I had the get-up-and-go to do the same, just to keep my mind off what I should do to get my children to visit more often. Calling and inviting them doesn't work, too much other stuff on their calendars.

An article in the morning newspaper starts my thinking. Before long, I arrive at a plan that just may jolt my daughter out of her lackadaisical attitude toward me. On Saturday morning, she has the machine take care of the phone calls while she does the laundry. I leave a message about her future. Next, I call the *Daily News,* tell them to have a reporter at the Williamsburg Parkway Bridge at one o'clock for an interesting story. Then I drive up to the bank.

Although the phone rings off the hook several times after I get back home, I do not answer it. At twelve-thirty, I leave the house, the sun bright, the air as clear as it used to be in my East Hampton days. I nestle the shoe box under my arm for the two-mile walk to the Parkway Bridge along a road lined with Norwegian maples. The tall, broad-leafed trees shade the walk nicely. Along the way, a Good Humor truck slows down next to me. I wave him on. Don't need the empty calories, delicious as they may be. I start humming "Rock of Ages."

I arrive at the bridge and start across over the highway. In the distance, from behind me, I hear a woman's breathless voice call out, "Mother, Mother. Don't do it." It's my daughter's voice. I knew she'd come.

Ignoring her, I hurry to the middle of the bridge. Above the noise of the traffic below, I shout, "Why not? Until you invest more time in me, I'll keep throwing it away."

I spew the contents of the shoe box down on the parkway below. Hundred dollar bills fly up, around, and down. Cars stop, a crowd gathers. Some of the bills land at my daughter's feet. The *Daily News* reporter takes pictures and picks up some of the bills, and we talk.

The next morning the *Daily News* carries the story about a woman teaching her daughter how to invest her time. My son now calls me occasionally to take me to brunch after Sunday Mass. And, weather permitting, my daughter joins me for a walk to the Parkway Bridge.

photo by Katie Utter

Pebbles and Crumbs
Ric Masten

last summer
whenever possible
my visiting granddaughter Cara
would worm her tiny hand into mine
and like Hansel and Gretel
we'd strike out from the house
up the "barking dog" trail
to the "creaky swings"—
don't you love the labels
little children put on things?—
and after a few "sky flying"
"watch me Grandpa" rides
it was on to the "sneaky table"
where hidden in the shade
beneath a giant live oak tree
we would split
the forbidden can of Coke I brought
   "damn it Dad her teeth will rot!"

rested and refreshed
we then ascend the "slidey steep"
to check the water level
in the "water keep"
to lift the lid and take a peek

then down the trail in single file we go
through the "witchy woods"
all the way to Arizona
which is what
my spouse has dubbed the shack
she uses as her dream shop and studio
Grandma it seems
also has a knack for naming things
    "if anyone calls
    tell them I'm in Arizona"

next stop—
the family memorial garden
where we solemnly commune with the trees
Kim and Emil have become
chanting softly as we pass
    "from ashes to ashes
    to flowering plum"

then wending our way
along a stretch of "dusty dirt"
we search for yesterday's footprints
covering them with today's
"backward walking" sometimes
    "to fool our enemies
    and friends"

and always during the final leg
of this backyard expedition
my companion lags behind—
little Miss Slowpoke
gathering specimens—
repeating after me the name
of every trailside shrub and tree
"eucalyptus—sticky monkey
lilac—sage—madrone"
and "don't touch that it's poison oak"
then suddenly—"we're home!"

last summer
Cara and I collected
and polished these moments
scattering them along the path
like pebbles
to be used in the distant future
the way a whiff of cigar smoke
brings my grandfather back
to poke about in the garden
with his walking stick
the way
my grandmother's face magically appears
at the taste of peppermint
her watchful presence close at hand
whenever I shake sand
from something that has been to the beach

I know
that on some faraway tomorrow
a sip of cola on a hot day—a pinch of sage
the creaking sound a rope swing makes—
these things with Cara's help
will bring me back to life again

and thankful as I am
for such life-extending crumbs
sadly I also know
that the cigar smoke and peppermint trick
can only be done by me—
in a couple of generations
it all becomes
a banquet for the crows

Rema
Sara Sanderson

Busy knitting the seasons,
she changes colors often.
Yarn flying, Grandmother crochets love,
    tying in treasures;
        miles of vibrant tapestry
finery feathered and furred,
jeweled with pine pitch,
dried moss,
emerald lake.
Seashore foam she flings into spirit,
swirled in her white-pine hair.
On wet sand,
in wolf prints,
she marks the way.

Instructions for Ashes
Ellen Kort

I will trust you to give away my turtle drum
rain stick   the redwood burl just beginning
to root   Return the borrowed books   old letters
hold me between thumb and forefinger   Drop
my ashes   dark as burnt paper   among chicory

alyssum   wild mint   Let me fall like sunlight
on irises unfolding purple wings   drop
blueward into sea   one salt crystal
the shell's secret core   Feed me

to summer trout   Let the hounds carry me home
through green gape of morning   a burdock
hooked tight   riding the fine mesh of fur
muscle and bone   falling in farmyards
rising up in the cow's small brown hills

crusted and dry   poked by a child's bare foot
Let me be welcome in folded leaves   cherry pit
appleseed   rose-colored moon inside the grape
If there is to be a eulogy   let it be

in the cloud of dust rising from hooves
a scar in some poet's hand   let it be
in riverbeds covered with snow   in the small talk
of birds   clam-colored light of early evening
Let it be one last milkweed pod   spitting seeds

What Faith Is
Lisa Vice

On Tuesday morning, my cat, Tommy, woke up, blinked his eyes in his slow deliberate way, but could not get down off the bed where he always sleeps, curled at my feet. When I lifted him to the floor, he stumbled lopsidedly like a drunk before he fell to his side, panting.

"It could be a brain tumor," the vet said, looking over my shoulder, as if he were addressing a ghost. "We see that sometimes in the old ones." Tommy lay in a heap on the table, crying pitifully, a terrified look in his eyes. With my hands on his thick orange fur, I felt him tremble and shake. I wanted to take him home, where I could press my face to his fur and talk to him properly. But the vet was saying something about tests, a chance of saving him, so I agreed to leave him overnight.

The next morning, the vet called to say he'd lost the cat. At first I took him literally, as if Tommy had gotten out of his cage, slipped out the door, and was on my doorstep right now, waiting for me to let him in.

"We can have him cremated," he was saying. Then I understood.

Every Wednesday, I have lunch with Doreen at The Monarch. Over egg salad sandwiches and iced tea, I tell her about the cat.

"From one day to the next, gone. Just like that." I have the sensation I am watching myself from a great distance. The sun is bright, shining directly into my face through the half-open slats of the blinds and I am glad for this. It gives me an excuse to squint and rub my eyes.

"Jean," Doreen says. "You can get another cat."

"I don't want another cat. I want Tommy. He wasn't just any cat."

"Maybe he was your child," Doreen says. "In a past life." Since Doreen went to that psychic fair at the community college, she's been talking this way, convinced she remembers sixteen of her past lives.

"Maybe," I say. Not that I agree, I just don't know what to say. Then I tell her something she wants to hear. "I have an interview."

Doreen's whole face lights up like a three-way bulb being flicked on, and the skin around her eyes crinkles into hundreds of folds. She squeezes my hand. I haven't worked in years, but I've been looking for a job since that day Doreen dropped by and found me in my pj's at three o'clock in the afternoon. She ran around pulling up the shades, saying, "You have to get a job or something. You need structure in your life."

So every morning I take a shower, comb my hair, then sit with the *Herald* folded open on my lap, circling possibilities: Front Desk Clerk. Bakery Sales. Receptionist. Cook.

"What's it for?" Doreen asks. My last interview was for an office worker-chimney sweep. I could see myself answering phones, swiveling in my chair to do some filing, then rushing off with a top hat on, climbing ladders, perched on a roof. Even though we both knew I was much too old to do such a thing, the young man who interviewed me had been very kind.

"A part-time innkeeper. Some kind of fancy bed and breakfast. But maybe I should cancel. I've got to do something with the cat."

"Do?" Doreen says. "Do? What are you talking about?"

"They said they'd cremate him. But I was reading in the paper how when they cremate your pet and give you a Baggy of ashes, it could be anybody's ashes. A Great Dane or a poodle or a Siamese. They just shove them all in together like it doesn't matter."

"What's all the fuss? The body's just a shell." Making comments like this is part of Doreen's psychic awakening. "It's like a chrysalis we crawl out of when our time comes." She waves up toward the ceiling where paper monarch butterflies dangle, decorating the restaurant.

Every year around this time, after traveling thousands of miles, the monarch butterflies make their way across the bay to rest in the pine and eucalyptus groves of our town. They fly slowly between the houses, exhausted from their journey. When I first moved here, I thought they would arrive in droves, the sky would darken, the air would fill with the sound of thousands of powdery wings fluttering by. But the butterflies actually drift along, alone or in pairs, buoyed by the autumn breeze.

"You and Nila were like husband and wife, Tommy's parents," Doreen is saying, dabbing at her lips with her napkin.

I choke a little on my tea. My heart thumps so loudly I'm sure Doreen can hear it. "Then you know?" I almost blurt, thinking maybe she really is psychic after all. "Did you always know?" I want to ask.

When Nila was alive, I used to tell her people loved us, they wouldn't turn their backs on us if they knew the truth. But she never wanted to risk it. "I'm not ashamed," she insisted. "I just like having our secret from the world."

"Of course you were roommates this time around." Doreen sucks the last of her tea through her straw. "But you acted just like an old married couple. Who knows? Maybe you were a king and queen on the Ivory Coast. Or an ordinary frumpy couple in Queen Victoria's England. A married couple, I'm sure of it. I wonder how I knew you then?"

My car is out front and after Doreen leaves, I get in it and drive toward Lighthouse Avenue. I took a special course for older drivers a few months ago. Not so much for the better insurance rates, but because I was having trouble. I'd make it to a stop sign, then not know what to do. I couldn't remember where I was headed or who had the right of way. Once I pulled in front of a police car, and he asked to see my license. Now I look ahead, watching for pedestrians, careful of the cars backing out of parking spaces in front of the bank and bookstore. Always ready to yield to the drivers inching forward from the blind intersections.

When I get home, I tell myself that Tommy is not going to rush to the window to greet me. But still as I unlock the door, I expect him to be there, rolling at my feet, offering his furry white belly. I look in the yellow pages and find the only pet cemetery is in Watsonville. I wonder what it involves to have a cat buried there. I wonder if there are headstones shaped like the pets buried under them. I can't imagine making the call. What would I say first? I sit on the sofa and stare at the ads on the page: Thor's Termite Control. Fleabusters. The Golden Dolphin Pet Shop. I read every word like it really matters to me.

I can hear the tick of the secondhand on my watch. I have another hour before my interview and my clothes are ready, so I lie back on the sofa. I keep thinking I see Tommy out of the corner of my eye, heading toward me. I have to restrain myself from calling out to him. Tommy would always come to me when I lay down. And when I wept he would creep slowly up my body until he rested on my chest, just under my chin.

"Tell me about yourself, while I read over your application," the owner of the inn says. I feel he has already dismissed me. I stare at my hands in my lap, the speech I prepared already fading. All I can think of is how I'm old enough to be his mother. I can hear Doreen in the back of my mind, urging me on, so I smile and speak as best I can.

"We do everything for our guests except polish their shoes," he tells me at one point. "Would you have trouble carrying a tray with champagne and an ice bucket up the stairs? There are a lot of stairs." Most of his questions begin with, "How would you rate yourself on a scale of one to ten, ten being the highest...?" Anything with numbers makes me panic but I take a deep breath. When he asks about my ability to make decisions, I announce in a loud voice, "Definitely a ten."

What must I have been thinking? Just trying to choose between spearmint gum or peppermint can leave me standing at the candy counter at Sprouse long enough for a line to form. But I have nothing to lose.

When I am leaving, a young woman wearing a thin white cotton blouse rushes up the stone steps, her sandals scraping the walk. I have an urge to wrap my arms around her. I am that hungry to touch. To be touched. I think of Nila murmuring into my hair, kissing my neck, her hands moving down my body, familiar as music. Would I really never feel this again? The thought takes my breath away. I lean against the stone wall watching the waves crash on the shore. A huge clipper ship, all the sails unfurled, glides like a mirage toward the harbor.

On the way home, I stop at the vet's. I'm still not sure what I'm going to do with Tommy. He is wrapped in a black garbage bag stuffed into the beige plastic cat carrier. It is unusually light as the boy hands it to me. Tommy was Nila's cat first, but I loved him too. I wonder what Nila would do now. I wonder what she would think if she could see me with a dead cat beside me on the front seat?

"Maybe I should have a Jewish funeral," Nila announced one night. She was driving us home from an Indian restaurant. I remember how it felt to sit in the dark car, to drive past the houses all lit up. I have no idea what prompted the discussion. Lord knows we were both old enough to be making such plans. But we'd never discussed it before. "I hate the idea of a stranger messing with my body after I'm dead," Nila said.

By the time we pulled up in front of the house, we'd both decided on cremation. It was fast, easy, and cheap. "Unless you buy a fancy urn," Nila said. I have often wondered if Nila had had a premonition. Like Doreen did when she dreamt of buildings crumbling the night before the Loma Prieta quake destroyed downtown Santa Cruz. Had she had a premonition? Or had she known all along and only pretended to be healthy? Pretended to be heading toward the future with me by her side?

When I get home, I take the cat out of his box. His body feels like an overripe tomato. I want to open the bag, but not right now. What I do is clear out the bottom of the refrigerator and put him inside. It's such a strange thing to do it actually cheers me up a little, and I take out a beer to help me think. Out the window three wild parrots fly by, their feathers bright green against the blue sky. They scream raucously, as if to tease the neighbor's parrot who screams back from the safety of its cage hanging beside the backdoor. I read somewhere that parrots outlive their owners. I wonder if this is how these three ended up swooping around town, resting on phone wires, calling from trees.

Nila had just celebrated her seventieth birthday. Seventy might seem old to some people, but it all depends on where you stand in relation to it. It seems young to me. But that's because I'm fifty-nine. Old? Ninety's old. But seventy? Nila was active right up to the end, riding her bike on the trails, hiking up Snively Ridge ahead of me.

When we first fell in love, Nila worried that if anyone found out what our relationship really was, she would lose her job. She was a children's librarian, after all. Imagine the scandal, she would say. So we let people think what they wanted all those years, never setting them straight. But when Nila died, nobody knew how to comfort me. They were surprised by the extent of my grief. "The money will be a big help," everybody said when they learned I was her beneficiary. "You can do whatever you want." As if this was what mattered. But it's not money I want. I want Nila. I want to wrap my arms around her soft waist and pull her close. I want to come home and find her on the sofa reading a book and lean over to kiss her. I want to walk down Pico Avenue, our shoulders brushing, our legs in rhythm, as we make our way to the sea.

The next morning, I am sure I feel a warm place by my feet where Tommy always lay. I imagine I hear the murmur of his purr. I get up quickly and go out to the kitchen. Even though there is the black plastic bag at the bottom of the refrigerator, I still reach for the can of cat food. Before I realize what I am doing, I have already filled his bowl. It sits on the counter while I sip my coffee. Outside the wind rattles the eucalyptus leaves. The sky seems to be clearing, the thick fog dispersing like wisps of smoke blowing out to sea.

I take the bag out of the refrigerator and untie the knot, pulling it open to look inside. And there he is. The familiar orange coat, the dark markings I loved to trace. I feel as if I'm unwrapping a fragile gift. There's my good boy. My Tommy, curled at the bottom as if asleep.

"Tommy," I say and pet the cold fur convinced if anyone saw me now they would never understand. They would think it morbid or even perverse. There is probably a law against it, but let them arrest me if they must. I've decided to bury Tommy out back. I put on my sneakers, get the shovel, and begin to dig in the far corner of the lot where Nila used to plant squash. The yard, always Nila's domain, is overgrown, a tangle of oxalis and marguerites choking the lavender and thyme. But the morning glories still climb up to the top of the porch like they have from the first year we bought the house and Nila planted them, fastening a trellis to the railing before the plants had more than two leaves.

"This is what faith is," she had laughed. It surprised us both when the flowers came back, year after year, planting themselves from the thick seed pods that fell to the ground, the vines reaching to the top of the steps, the bright purple blossoms cascading like a waterfall.

As I dig, I have this picture in my mind, as clearly as if I'm watching it projected on a screen. There is Nila in her nightgown, so small, her face deathly pale. I am beside her wishing she would say something, wishing she would open her eyes, give my hand an answering squeeze. One morning she sat up in bed, coughed, and her hand filled with blood. In a week her skin was as translucent as rice paper.

How I wish Nila were with me now, sitting in the red chair, watching me scoop the dark soil into a pile. I pry out a large stone and continue digging, moving rhythmically, as if to the steps of a dance, until the hole is deep enough so that years later, when someone else lives in our house, they won't unearth the bones.

There's a box under the house, just the right size. But first I wrap Tommy in his favorite blanket. Doreen has told me how in one of her past lives she was Egyptian. She was entombed with all her favorite possessions for her journey to the other side. I think of this now as I put in a fur mouse and a crocheted ball, along with a handful of treats, heart-shaped nuggets Tommy loved so much he would stand on his hind legs for one. I fit the box into the hole and scatter soil onto it. The soil makes a thumping sound, then it's just soil on soil, and I pack it down, push it down tight, not wanting the raccoons to come nosing around.

Dust to dust. The words of the funeral come back to me. It's not an end but a beginning. The voices singing "Holy, holy, holy." I remember how Nila and I used to stand in that church, Sunday after Sunday, year after year, side by side, never touching, afraid of offending someone. But in private we had wrapped our arms around each other.

My body is unused to the work I have done. My back aches and my fingernails are crusted and black, but I feel good as I sit on the back steps. I pray, as I have so many times, that Nila will forgive me. She died believing we were the only ones who knew. But the nurse at the hospital had understood. This I am sure of. She never thought for a moment that we were sisters or roommates. She always pulled the curtain to give us privacy and never came around it without stopping first to say a few words to the Italian lady who lay complaining in the other bed. She spoke loudly, as if warning us she was on her way.

When Nila died, I crawled onto the bed, pulling her into my arms. The nurse left me this way for a long time, even wheeled Mrs. Manetti down to the solarium where the TV blared. When she came back, she put her hands on my shoulders. She was a big woman who stood tall in her white pantsuit. She patted my back, murmuring, "I know. I know."

Then she brought towels and a washbasin of steaming water and left me alone. She'd understood, without saying anything, without asking, the way nurses understand the need for mothers of newborns to unwrap the swaddled babies and check every inch. I washed the familiar fingers, the scar on Nila's left palm where she'd cut herself on a broken glass, reaching into the dishpan. The bit of stone embedded in her knee that her mother had said would eventually work its way out. But skin had grown over it instead. I ran the warm cloth across the knobs of her spine, the smooth bones of her ribs, around the mole on her left shoulder and up the back of her neck, my hands sweeping her thick white hair aside. I washed her feet. Monkey feet I called them, and Nila would laugh and use her toes to turn on the radio, to pick pens up off the floor. I washed her, her skin as soft as crepe, and remembered the first time we kissed. How it had felt like coming home.

On the other side of the fence, my neighbor begins to rake his yard. His parrot, excited to have company, reaches its beak through the cage for a kiss. "What kind of bird are you?" the man asks. "What kind of bird are you?"

"I'm a lucky dog. Lucky dog," the parrot squawks. "Where's the cat? Here kitty kitty." Then it does an imitation of a police siren and begins its litany again.

I sit on the steps and think to myself: I loved a woman. And I am glad for this. I try not to regret all the times I never touched her in public. Not even when we were so old it didn't matter. Two old women hand in hand, what's the big deal?

Down in the weeds I see something move. It's a monarch butterfly struggling to fly. I think maybe it's injured and I should try to help, but as I watch, it spreads its wings. They are bright as stained glass, soft as velvet. I watch it lift itself up with great effort, and then I see, clutched in its tiny legs, another butterfly, its wings folded like hands in prayer, hanging beneath as they glide up over the fence.

Doreen would say it is a sign and I suppose it is, but I don't want to think about what it means. Instead I think how in a few minutes I will go inside and sit on the sofa with the newspaper. I will circle all the ads for jobs I will not get. I will not be a baby-sitter. Will not earn four hundred dollars a month delivering newspapers in my spare time. Will never fix anyone's car or drive a school bus. The idea of this makes me feel light-headed, almost giddy, as I head inside.

What do old women talk about if they don't talk about aches and pains and ill health?
Eunice Holtz

They talk about sunsets and the schedules of the moon, about chickadees and goldfinches at the feeder, and they check their bird books to identify the female rose breast-ed grosbeak, and they name one female cardinal "Emily" because it's the most beautiful name Edna can think of.

They talk about the changing view from the second floor, north window, about the profusion of impatiens growing outside the door, about the Deerfield girl's basketball team—win or lose it's for fun and teamwork.

They talk about the delightful flavor of the vegetable medley served the night before, about the lack of Queen Anne's lace growing this year, about the garter snake's comings and goings from under the foundation of the garage.

They talk about the long life of a pet tarantula and they sit and watch in amazement as it sheds its skin again.

And they talk about volunteering at schools and for Habitat for Humanity.

And they remind each other to stop and listen to the wind in the tall pines across the road.

They talk about words—words for crossword puzzles and Scrabble—and they always keep a dictionary handy to check on meanings.

They share Bible verses that fit current situations.

They share photos of parties and grandchildren and places they've been and they share student notes from recent Elderhostels.

They talk about potted plants and Edna teaches us to watch for the most amazing star within a star, within yet another star of her blooming hoya.

They talk about the positive, and when war and suffering need to be mentioned they remind each other to trust in God's power, still.

They talk about the delight of the changing seasons and they race to tell each other, on certain white winter mornings, to look quickly at the newly frosted world.

They talk of nieces and nephews and of the loving attention they've received from them.

They talk of their children and thank God for their capabilities and thank God for the richness the children bring.

They are quick to report the first sounds of the first spring peepers and they find it worth talking about when they hear the strange calls of the great horned owl as the young one begs food from its mother.

What do old women talk about? When they care about nature and all things bright and beautiful, they never run out of things to talk about.

But after saying all that, I must say, most of all they share a love of silence.

They know it's in silence they can hear best and learn most.

photo by Teresa Tamura

Retrospective Eye
Katherine Govier

Christopher "Tyke" Ditchburn tiptoed past a piano draped with a Spanish shawl, between stacks of books and prints, and over the spare handwoven rug, intending to switch on the lamp. Seated in the darkness in a mission-style chair was Miss Ditchburn herself. So he thought of her today, as Miss Ditchburn. Erect, she stared fixedly into the winter garden. Her hair was thick and white, short as a man's; her neck was lined and thin, her hands lay motionless in her lap.

"Tyke?" The voice was deep and dry. "I know you're there. No use trying to surprise me."

He reached the lamp and pulled the thin chain. A cone of amber light fell over her lap. The shade was made of tiny gold beads of glass from the island of Murani, in the shallow basin of seawater off Venice. He knew its story as well as he knew his own. The house, the garden, her few treasures: he had come to think of them as his own.

She was nearly blind now, the great photographer. Old age had done that. Her sharpness, however, was undiminished. Impatience, selfishness, hauteur, stronger than ever. That she had agreed to work with him on the retrospective was something of a minor miracle. How Tyke had got lucky, when Professors Sullivan and Moore had been refused—though they were responsible, in part, for her current high standing—he did not know. Of course she was his mother, but that had never counted for much.

"I guess my timing is right," Tyke had said over the telephone grimly. "She keeps promising to die." And the curator had frozen in the midst of her victory leap in her Bloor Street apartment, to stand dismayed: Does Corinne Ditchburn's son hate her? More important, now that she's agreed, she can't go and die on us. Not on the Royal Ontario Museum of Art.

"I wasn't trying to sneak up." He trod more noisily on the hardwood and put out a hand. The old woman, hard and forbidding and determined, even the line of her arm as it reached for him, seemed to scour him with her unclouded grey eyes. Yet he never knew if she really saw him.

So he's it, Cory thought. At the end of my life, my son the cod has come to record my confession. Why does he look like a cod? Or is he a flounder? I ate one, alive, in Yokohama; it was impaled on spikes at either end and the sides were sliced. So tender with green mustard. She smiled inadvertently. At least I can hardly see him. I'll keep my eyes on the light in the garden, watch how the day lengthens into spring.

"So you're it."

"I'm it," said Tyke. "No, actually you're it. I'm merely the means."

If I could stomach that, I can stomach anything. Now all I have to stomach is myself, since I've decided to do this thing. I said no for a long time. I said no whenever I thought they were interested in me because of Albert

Bloom, whenever they said "pupil of..." I said no because I was not a war photographer. I said no. But look. Vanity wins out in the end. Vanity and the need to—

She sought for the words to justify herself to herself. Words were not her medium. Not justify. Not explain. *See.* The need to see it all, one more time.

"Where do we begin?"

"There will have to be a brief biography."

"Whatever for?" snapped Cory. "This is about my work. I didn't agree for you to exhibit my life, only my work."

"We'll leave that then," he said.

He pulled the cords which lowered the blinds, Levolor blinds which could be left down, the angle adjusted by twirling a plastic wand, but which she insisted on yanking up to the very top of the windows. Before she could complain he went on.

"The photographs have arrived from Del Zotto, Barr," he said. "I've got them all in boxes here. We'll have a look through." He drew out a pair of soft white cotton gloves, and pulled them over his hands.

She had never liked this reverence. Loose, the gloves made his hands cartoony, the hands of a Mickey Mouse. Or sinister, like the hands of a surgeon, someone who performed an autopsy, thought Cory. Forensic surgeon.

He cleared the pine table, long, made of one piece of wood, which had been his grandmother Eliza Ditchburn's pride. With his softly gloved white hands, he opened the first of the large black-latched boxes. Carefully, he lifted the white cardboard folder and put it on the table. He opened it. The thin veiling paper lay over the print.

"I've sorted all the prints and all the negatives starting with the thirties. But I'd like you to look at them, just to be sure they're what we think they are. Can you see, in this light?"

It depended on her mood. She was like the deaf man who won't answer when spoken to but hears a whisper across the room.

"I haven't looked at those in forty years."

Delicate fingered, he slid the large exhibition prints toward her. "Here's what it says," he said, reading.

Fig. 1.
Corinne Ditchburn
Epiphany Fire in Chelsea,
London 1937.
Gelatin silver. 34 x 23 cm.

"It's mounted. Must have been shown before, in New York."

Cory put her long, tendon-striped forearms on the table. Under the light, her face pulled up close to its surface, she scanned the photograph, side to side, up and down. As if she were herself a beam of light, searching, as if she could sense what lay on the paper by exposing her face to it.

Oh, my. That fire. How I loved it. All fires. On the island, burning garbage in old oil drums. Bonfires on the rocks, the orange flames feasting on inky air. When the fire was hot enough, the rocks beneath would crack, making a sound like gunshots.

Perhaps I am an incendiary. Didn't I thrive on explosions? Beginning with the lightning that flung its brilliant web across the Northern Ontario sky, and the small wait, that silence, the intake of breath between light and sound. Praying time: how far away is it? One mile, two miles, three miles, then great bear's growl of thunder.

When I discovered the camera, it was that little explosion that captivated me. An explosion of light on an emulsion of silver bromide, a chemical bath. The shutter went, the black surface of paper was exposed for its split second to the glare of day. And an image bloomed in the blackness.

At first, the landscape was not damaged by these explosions: it still stood. It had been borrowed from, it had been reproduced. I owned the small explosion, I set it, I saw by it. For that fraction of a second when the flash went off, I was blinded, lost. Life stopped. I did not blow anything up. I had merely created. Afterward, there it was: the same landscape, unaltered, except as it would alter normally, the sun having moved a little along its path, the bicycle having rolled out of view, the wind having bent the tree.

It was only later that my camera exploded everything I pointed it at.

Before I ever went to war, I dreamed of explosions. At the munitions plant, those cordite straws that went through my hands, which I cut, and selected, and bundled would, when packed into a shell or a bomb, not stop, but propel the world. I thought of it that way, as a reaction of gases and solids, as a wave, pushing outward, turning darkness into light.

I loved the acrid smell of the cordite, and I loved the men and women who labored over it, the welders who went down into the tanks to mend the breaks in the cast iron. When they lit their torches it was an invitation to disaster. We blessed our foreheads with nitroglycerin every day we didn't work, to keep up our exposure. If we didn't, the headaches came. Crumbled cordite was shed all over the plant; we wore it like stardust.

We never thought we were making death. Not until the night the TNT shed exploded, and in the darkness I searched the runoff ditch for bodies. And when I found one—my first war casualty in Nobel, Ontario—my first instinct was to raise the camera, to capture him. Take him prisoner.

When I went to war, the camera protected me. I wore it like a shield in the face of overwhelming danger. If I was not immune, then I was especially charged, with a task, a name. I was there, Kilroy, my name scrawled on the wall. Corinne Ditchburn pressed this shutter. Despite massed armies, razed cities, fleeing millions, I stopped time for that split second.

Tracer bullets make a white arc on the black sky, as if a razor has sliced the dome and let in a hairline of heaven. When bombs hit, it's so bright that your eyes go black. When you open them, seconds or maybe years later, you only see white—smoke, dust, rubble, refractions. Sound travels more slowly, ricocheting from stone walls and mountainsides, being buried here, echoing there, arriving at last disconnected from its origin. So, blind, deaf, you crouch in the low-ceilinged world below explosions. Some new world is being born overhead, licked with fire, swaddled in smoke and thunder. You are a creature of mud and ooze, a worm. You lie awaiting death, expecting it, even hoping for it, wanting something quick, manageable, a respite. More terrifying is to know that you will not die, that when the darkness seeps off, the smoke has blown past, and the world you knew is gone, you will pick up your dead, and begin again.

Cory came awake in the dark of Toronto winter's early evening; she'd slept through tea time. Her pelvis had been rocked by some spasm, some recollection. Passion, that old dog that barked at her door now only in dreams. Nagging her: had it been a misspent life, after all? Perhaps she ought to have been, as Albert suggested, an anatomist of the senses. "You should be making love for a living," he told her once. And later, when she refused him: "I can't understand why you've given it up."

The sun had come through the January clouds that afternoon, exposing one by one the naked limbs of the birch, the lilac, the flowering crab. Sudden beauty was the best kind, sudden and brief, split second. It ambushed the barricades and twisted the heart. The sun often came through at the end of the day in London, too. That was its final joke, after you'd dashed in sloppy buckets of rain all day, from awning to awning, dodging the points of umbrellas.

"London's like that," Albert would say. "The end of things is best here. The end of summer, the end of the year. The end of each life. Don't you agree?"

"Don't you go getting valedictory on me," she'd said.

She leaned over the pine tool chest that her grandfather had made. He was a fair carpenter, it was always said of the man, who worked on the ships at Parry Sound in winter, caught rheumatoid arthritis and died at forty-four. Once the box had been filled with handmade planes, but she'd given those away, to Tyke. Now it held boxes of photographs, shots which she hadn't published, hadn't shown to Del Zotto, Barr, hadn't even shown to Tyke.

She was looking for a picture of Tyke on the rocks in front of the Ojibway, taken the day she came home from Europe. She dragged the book to where she could see. Perhaps this was it. But what she recalled—her son's shy joy, his little torso bursting with heart, his chin up so that his face became a dish of pure sun—was now only light and shadow.

"Don't you think it's interesting, what life has done to me?" she challenged Tyke, only yesterday, wasn't it?

"Interesting? Not the word I'd use, Mother. See how you distance yourself? Even from your own tragedy?"

The blindness, what was it? Nothing more than a further development of her seeing. Narrowing down. Winnowing out. She had to look at it that way, as part of the process, not as an ambush, in later years. She reduced people, yes. What artist didn't, to make a statement? This is not Tyke, she said to him when he protested her depictions of him; this is a photograph of Tyke; it is an analog. Not the you you are, or choose to be. But an occasion for my *saying* you, for what I say about you.

She remembered him facing the camera in a thin T-shirt and cut-off shorts, but naked really, his collarbone visible, sharply curved like the jawbone of a fish, his eye sockets hollow, a wild animation in his smile, a feverish happiness dampened, there in the eyes, by early wisdom. His body so taut and tender. There was nothing extra, just his sun-burned buttery blond skin with its white boy-hairs; his shoulders, strong for his age and rounded, not angular, but almost chiseled. The sun had loved him, it followed him, lasted in his eyes, in his laugh, on his shoulders, after it had gone from the water and the rocks. She'd seen statues in Italy like him. But they had been wrapped in sacking against the bombs.

Later, Tyke refused to let her photograph him. Said she was stealing his life, he did. She hadn't understood.

But now he was stealing hers.

Retrospective! Who wanted to look back? And who could afford it? Her mother used to quote Pope: "In vain the Sage, with Retrospective eye, would from the apparent What conclude the Why."

When she told that to Tyke he laughed: "Mother you're so secretive! For an exhibitionist, especially," he protested. "Who lived her life in public. Made everyone else public." But if she let go of all the threads of her life, if she let them all know her secrets, she would no longer belong to herself. She would be their creature. And she had never wanted to belong to anyone but herself.

What she wanted was to find that sun-blessed boy again. She wanted to tell him she was sorry, she wished she hadn't left him. (Yet she had to leave him; she would not be who she was if she hadn't left him.) Somehow, she hadn't understood that his life, too, had its imperatives,

148

that he couldn't stand still and wait for her wars and assignments and dates with whatever destiny.

If she could catch him off guard, surprise him again, as she'd done that day. He'd run up the rocks as he did then, and she would hold out her arms and call, "Tyke!" the cameras slapping at her side.

The Well
Christopher Woods

Forget, for the moment, the women who gather there talking, waiting to fill pitchers. And forget for now the dirty-faced children who twist their mother's skirts, who spit at one another, and who toss laughter wildly in the air. Forget all that.

What matters now is this one man, bent and nameless, who has slowed there, so close to the well. For him, now, even walking has become a curse. What he thinks about as he walks is the agony that, until now, he has resisted thinking about. Breathing deeply, he swallows one child's laugh, then another.

Slowly he circles the well, feels it pulling him into its bosom. Nearby, sitting on benches, are other old men. Maybe they have been there forever. He remembers running past them when he was still a child.

He never had time to stop, to talk to them. Or as a man in middle age, passing but not really seeing them. And later, his own hair and beard white, he had looked away rather than think about them. He would have no part of all that.

Until now. He circles until he finds a place to sit. He is lucky. The bench is still warm from someone else. He wonders whose place he has taken, where they have gone. Away for a few minutes? For eternity? And he wonders how long he will remain there, within the pull of the well, the lure of its depth. All that.

Maybe, he thinks, it won't be so bad. Feeding on the circular darkness that grows out of the earth. Watching children passing, the older men who look away. Even the other tired old men who stand so near to the well, all of them waiting patiently for a seat.

Retired
Daniel Green

When he could no longer work he sat
bewildered, wondered what he was supposed
to do, his work was life, his life, work,
he felt undone, bereft of being the man
he used to be, a cracked stone jug, empty.

Bringing home a workman's pay was his
solid base of dignity, responsibility fulfilled,
the roles of husband, father, guide, and judge,
earned and justified.

Even pensions, truly earned, did not qualify
as pay. Tolerance was not a substitute
for respect. His opinions about the day's events
were not asked, took comfort in soliloquy.

The tasks at home he'd never done became
the day's routines—at kitchen sink, supermarket,
shuffling behind the vacuum cleaner,
hanging wash, all women's work—he learned,
resigned to do with grace.

He thought he'd earned for keeps the badge
of "Mister," but that, too, slipped away,
became a thoughtless "Pops," a nothing name.

Emmaline
Willa Holmes

Emmaline's cheeks felt hot. Surely they were flushed and he would notice. She steadied her fingers against the handle of the coffee pot.

"Want some more coffee?" Her voice sounded high and funny to her, but if Howard marked the difference, he didn't let on.

"No," he said. "I've got to be on my way. I promised Roger I'd stop by the office and show them how I handled the Newton account. Then I'll get a haircut."

Retirement hasn't changed him, she thought. Keeps time better than a clock.

"The salesmen down at the office really think I've got it made, coming and going as I please." Howard gulped his orange juice and dipped egg yolk off his plate with a last bit of toast. "When you go out, pick up my cleaning, will you? It's two suits and a sports jacket. Oh, and take my black shoes in for new heels. I left them out next to the bed. I'll be back home by twelve-thirty for lunch."

Emmaline carried the dishes to the sink and lowered them into hot soapy water. Howard didn't think it was worth getting a dishwasher for just the two of them.

"Why don't you let the dishes soak while you go up and make the bed?" Howard said. "More efficient that way."

"I've done it this way for years," she said.

"Just trying to be helpful, Emmy." She watched him go out the backdoor and down the driveway toward the car.

"He hasn't called me Emmy since Dora and Tim were little," she thought. Then she stiffened her back. "Won't make any difference." She put the last cup into the drainer and squeezed water out of the dishrag. She stretched it out over the edge of the sink to dry. Funny to think she wouldn't be there to use it again. To wash the lunch dishes or the dinner dishes.

"Won't be any lunch. Or dinner, either," she said aloud to the kitchen. When the phone rang, she knew it'd be Addie. Addie'd come over or called almost every day for the ten years she'd lived next door.

"Morning, Em," Addie said. "How's it going?"

"Hard," Emmaline answered.

"Changed your mind?"

"No. Yes. I don't know. What should I do, Addie?"

"I told you what I thought. Have it out with him. Tell him that big house is too much for you now, and having him in and out all day is driving you crazy."

"Wouldn't do any good. He doesn't hear what I say."

"Well, then, what's it to be?"

"I don't know. The house. Howard. It's hard to leave. And I've been patient, haven't I? Patient with all his ways?"

"Of course, you have. You've got the best, most patient disposition of anyone I know. In fact, if you'd just get mad once in a while..."

"That's not my way. And it's not Howard's way to be any different than he is." She stood, holding the phone. Then: "I'll do it. I'll move to my new place today, just like I planned."

"Are you sure? I don't know how you can live in a rent-ed room. Not after having your own house and all."

"I'm sure. Anyway, it's a one-room apartment. There's that little kitchenette in what used to be a closet. I thought I'd put up a drape so I can pull it closed if somebody comes. So they couldn't see the dirty dishes."

"You with dirty dishes? That's not like you."

"Maybe it will be."

Em took off her apron and looked in the hall mirror, fluffing up her grey hair. Best get going before Howard comes back. She reached into the hall closet for a light beige coat and a small suitcase, the same one she'd packed with clean nightgowns for herself and with baby clothes and diapers for the new baby the two times she'd gone to the hospital.

"Time to get out of here," she told the hall. She shifted the suitcase to one side as she closed the door and twisted the knob to make sure it locked. She'd picked the day care-fully. She rented the room over the bakery nearly a month before, but she waited to make the move on the day she knew Dora would be driving in to go to the dentist and to spend the rest of the afternoon with them.

The clock in the room over the bakery ticked so loudly she turned and looked at it. Two o'clock. By now Howard had come home and found no lunch waiting. Dora was through with her appointment with the dentist and had walked up the steps to the front porch. Would Howard be standing there, looking down the street, fuming because lunch was late? Or would he be sitting at the kitchen table, waiting for her to come rushing in, apologizing for the delay, taking mayonnaise and sandwich meat out of the refrigerator and bread from the bread box on the counter?

They wouldn't call the police, would they? Not this soon. Would Dora think to call Addie, to see if she knew where her mother was?

Emmaline told Addie, "Just Dora. If it's Howard that calls or comes over, don't tell. Just Dora."

The rocking chair creaked beneath her. Been hard to get it out of the house. She'd waited until after dark on the night Howard went to lodge meeting. Addie'd backed her son's pickup to the garage door. Emmaline had gathered together all the things she planned to take to the new place and covered them with a tarp at the back of the garage. Howard didn't go in there much since he'd hurt his back and hired a yard man to mow the grass.

The ticking of the clock matched the creaking of the stairs. Someone was coming. She turned the rocker away from the window and faced the door, rocking faster, in time with the ticking and the creaks.

She waited for the raps on the door. "Mom? Mom, are you in there?" Dora's voice sounded anxious.

"I'm here. Come on in."

The door swung open and Dora pushed in past it. "Are you all right? Has something happened?"

"Didn't Addie tell you?"

"She said where I could find you is all. And not to bring Dad. Have you two had a fight?"

"No. Nothing like that. Sit down. Take that chair at the table by the window. Remember it? It was your Grandma Rose's. I found it up in the attic when..."

"You've been planning this? You've been going through the attic looking for things to bring here? This is—*premeditated*?" Dora's voice grew shrill.

"It's OK, Dora. Really it is. Sit down and I'll explain."

Dora pulled the chair out into the room and sat down in it, fanning her face with her hand. "Really, Mom, this is crazy. It's just insane."

Emmaline recoiled inside. She hadn't imagined they'd think she was crazy. They couldn't make her go home, could they?

"How will you get along? How will you manage?" Dora's face was red and she looked as if she'd cry.

"I'll do just fine," Emmaline told her. "I've got it all figured out. As a matter of fact, that's what made up my mind for me. Your father took me down to the Social Security office before he retired. They had me sign papers, too, both of us about to be sixty-five."

"But just because you get Social Security..."

"Don't you see? A separate check came to me. It had my name on it. I never knew they did it that way. Howard had me endorse the first check, and he put it in the bank. That's when I knew."

"Knew what, Mom?"

"I knew that check was mine. It was meant for me. I went back to that office and put in a change of address as soon as I found this room." She sat up straighter. "I have my own income."

"But what if it isn't enough to live on? Dad has a retirement fund, a pension plan. You'd be so much better off." She looked around the room and frowned. "If you're really going through with this, Dad'll probably have to give you money."

"Either way, I'll be all right," Emmaline said, smoothing her skirt across her legs. "They told me at that government office how much money I can earn before they take away part of my check. Mrs. Morgan in the bakery downstairs says I can work behind the counter for her Monday and Wednesday mornings. And I've already found a baby-sitting job two nights a week, but I told them I don't do housework and I don't do dishes."

Dora pulled the hair back off her face. "What am I going to tell Dad?"

"Tell him..." Emmaline paused, but for just a second. "Tell him I've retired."

A Free Man
Judith Bell

Part determination, part habit, Bradford Clemmons jostled his way through the press of commuters waiting for the city-bound train on the platform outside Melmont station. He liked being up front, leaning out over the tracks, keeping watch on the point in the distance where the parallel lines of the rails seemed to narrow, the cross ties disappearing. There was something about that first sighting of the train rolling out of a still languorous morning haze, its great round light sweeping clear the way into the city, making him feel life was right on course.

But this morning his eyes strayed from that particular bend in the track, wandered over the people keeping watch beside him. Not that he knew any of them. They were mostly the ages his children would be if he had any, and he tended to see them as such. The number of his peers catching this train had steadily dwindled these last few years, leaving him to feel like the last hanger-on.

His immediate neighbors had all retired long ago. He saw them on his way to the station each morning, puttering among their flowers, walking their dogs, padding down the flagstones in slippers and robe for the morning paper. He pictured them going back inside, having that second cup of coffee, and then being lost, totally lost, the way he found himself on Sunday afternoons. After the paper had been read section by section, a televised golf tournament watched—he'd never had the time to take up the sport—Bradford was ready to be back at the office, away from the calm and quiet of his own house. "Your problem," Jen, his wife, liked to say, "is that you equate leisure with idleness."

"Brad!"

Bradford ignored the call. No one but Jen called him Brad anymore, and she was so busy with her painting, with the children's art classes she taught, it was possible she hadn't noticed how the name no longer fit him, how, with his expanded midsection and achromatic hair—no longer black, not exactly grey—he had settled into the solidity of the uncle for whom he'd been named.

"Hey, Brad!"

There it was again, sounding insistently in his direction. He looked further down the platform, stared with contextual blindness at a young man waving his newspaper at him. Why, it was Davis Thurman from his accounting firm. What was Thurman doing in an established community like Melmont? Of course Bradford was only twenty-two when he moved here, but he had been married with a baby on the way.

He remembered driving down street after street of Colonials, Tudors, and Victorians built in the 1920s and 1930s, chafing against the suburb's settledness. He'd grown up in old Richmond in a sprawling Victorian maze of dark rooms. Up North, out on his own, he developed a decided preference for the impermanent, the new. "My husband likes subdivisions," Jen had offered to the real estate agent in explanation of his silence.

"If it's any comfort, Melmont was built by developers. Of course, after thirty years houses take on an unavoidable grace." The agent let them into a fieldstone house she affectionately referred to as "the Irish cottage." "Natural air-conditioning," she offered when Bradford complained about the outdated kitchen, the oil furnace. Jen ran her hand along the deep windowsills, traced the molding in the casement windows. Pregnant, she had taken on a new vulnerability, a softness that made him rush to please her. And he could see she wanted this house with an intensity of desire he was only capable of feeling for her.

Bradford sensed the agent watching him watch his wife's face flush with pleasure as she traced the toe of her sandal delicately along the pattern in the parquet floor. "It's a quick walk to the station, a thirty-minute ride to Grand Central. And remember, Melmont is small, it lacks name recognition. Prices here will be a full twenty percent lower than Scarsdale or Larchmont."

"We'll take it," Bradford had said, grateful she had continued to appeal to his practical side even after seeing his weakness.

"Brad." Thurman was suddenly beside him. "Thought you'd thrown in the towel, old man." He cuffed Bradford's shoulder, offered his hand for shaking. "Just closed on a condo." He pointed his paper in the direction of the commercial district.

"Yes, the condos, of course." They were considered an eyesore by residents of Bradford's neighborhood, Melmont Manor. Thurman wore the uniform sported by all the young additions to the firm: khaki pants, navy blazer, loafers. Like them, he expended a great deal of energy on putting himself on equal footing with the senior staff. It wasn't enough that they took the liberty of calling you, uninvited, by your first name, they went further, as if by shortening your name they could make you less substantial, less of an obstacle.

"So anyway, hey," Thurman tapped him with his newspaper, "you're a free man. So what are you doing here with the working stiffs?"

Bradford repositioned himself to resume watch, but young Thurman, who had the bulk of a boy who had not that long ago excelled at college ball, moved with him. "I've been taking this train for forty years. I always promised myself the day after I retired I was going to get dressed, walk to the station, wait for the train, watch the rest of you get on, watch the train pull out, and go home."

"That's wild," Davis said, which was what he seemed to say about everything. Bradford wondered if this was a pat phrase among athletes like "There you go!" had been in his college days, and the not knowing made him feel his age. He waited for Davis to say something more, but judging from the pleasantly blank look in his eyes, he would not.

"Why aren't you playing pro ball, Thurman?" Bradford said, shifting the focus of the conversation from himself. "My hunch is right, you did play in school, didn't you?"

Davis sucked in a middle just beginning to soften. "That's right. Quarterback, Penn State. Knees." He looked down, buckling his joints slightly. "Lost it all in one sack. Wild, huh? Hey, there's the train."

"So it is," Bradford said, irritation edging into his voice

at having his ritual upset.

"Have a nice retirement," Davis waved his paper over his head, stepped through the doors opening in front of them and disappeared, digested by a shifting mass of grey and blue suits. The commuters around Bradford surged forward, and he found himself caught in the undertow. Familiar morning smells greeted him inside the car: coffee, aftershave, perfume, mouthwash. He breathed deeply, overriding the catch in his throat. It would be so easy to wait for the conductor's call of "All aboard," to yield to the backward press of the crowd as the doors closed, to adjust to the list and sway of the car as the train pulled out of the station. He could stay here unnoticed, anchoring his attaché case between his legs, holding his folded newspaper in front of his face.

The specter of Grand Central Station came to mind. He saw the passengers fan out, absorbed by the larger crowd, all of them with a destination, a place they belonged. Even the panhandlers at Grand Central had a reason to be there. The prospect of facing his own aimlessness sent him hurtling toward the Melmont platform.

"Coming out," he cried, his voice lost in the screech of the conductor's whistle. He stopped the meeting of the doors with his attaché case, landed on the platform. Free of the train, he watched it glide out of the station, silver and perfect, the faces of the passengers forming a band of unbroken color behind the seamless ribbon of glass.

"You miss your train?" A young man in a custodial uniform emptied the ashtray beside Bradford.

Yes, Bradford thought, watching the custodian drop the

bowl of the ashtray roughly in its holder, *I do miss my train.* Instead he said in the hearty voice he used for talking to other men, "Retired just yesterday. Thought I'd come down, watch the rest of them hit the grind."

"Man, this is the last place I'd be if I was retired."

"Where would you be?" Bradford waited, ready to endow the impending answer with revelatory meaning.

The custodian tapped the end of a cigarette he took from his shirt pocket against the back of his hand, lit it. "I'd be on some island, man, Jamaica maybe, sitting on the beach, doing nothing."

"So you'd travel?"

The custodian flicked ashes into the ashtray he'd just emptied. "Yeah, sure. People's all through expecting you to do things. Time to do something for yourself."

Bradford shifted his gaze to a splashy poster announcing an art exhibition that had just opened at the Met. He could look for Jen at the art center where she taught two days a week. They'd go into the city, look at things he hadn't taken the time to see, do the things she'd given up trying to share with him.

He tried to think of when she had first changed, when she gave all the attention she'd focused on him—on the babies she'd never managed to carry to term—to her art instead, to her students, transforming her pleas for closeness and understanding into unreadable blobs and smears of paint. After one of her trips to the doctor, he had come home to find her in tears, furiously rolling white paint over the yellow walls in the room they had intended as a nursery. "This is my studio," she'd announced, wiping her eyes with the back of her fist, smearing paint across her face. "If I can't create physically, I'll create esthetically."

At first she had simply invited neighbor children in to play at making art, but he put his foot down after coming home one day to find the lower half of the back of the house transformed into a giant mural of flowers and trees and hovering butterflies, the porch columns ribboned with paint. Watching him scrub her afternoon's work away, Jen never argued once. She had simply set about organizing support for a community art center in the old Laury School behind the post office.

Outside the station, the sun blasted him with a directness unfamiliar to a man accustomed to spending his days in an office building. Shielding his eyes, he rushed past storefronts, imagining idle shopkeepers watching him, speculating about his business in town on a Thursday morning.

Climbing the steps to the Laury Art Center he noticed they were beginning to crumble, that paint peeled from the windows and gutters Jen and her volunteers had painted a cheery red. Day lilies just past their bloom bordered the walk. Donated and planted by the local nursery, the failing blossoms drooped forward into beds choked with weeds. What could Jen be thinking of, walking past this neglect day after day? She had never managed to pick up that life was serious business, that there were things that had to be attended to. Whatever fool thing she or "the children" as she referred to her students, took into their heads to do was all that mattered to her. She didn't see the clutter that began in her studio, inched its way into the hallway, the spare bedroom, and beyond; she didn't notice the disrepair of the art center and what's more, she seemed to pride herself on this failing.

From the door of the airy classroom where she taught her preschoolers, he watched her, dressed in jeans and a paint-smeared denim shirt, crawl from the work of one child to another. She stopped to retie the ribbon holding back her straggling grey hair. In her flushed face he was surprised to see the fresh beauty he'd remembered just this morning, thinking of her and the day they'd first looked at their house. She was the same as she had always been, all her life building on that moment when she had the courage to paint the nursery walls white. In comparison his own life felt segmented, compartmentalized, and now, abruptly broken.

"Brad!" Smiling, Jen scrambled to her feet, clapped her hands. "Children, look who's here. Mr. Clemmons has come to look at the worlds you've made."

A boy charged into Bradford's legs, leaving a brown hand print on his trousers. "I'm drawing a planet with chocolate rivers and silver trees. What's yours like?"

"What a great idea, Simon! You come make something, too, Brad." Jen took his attaché case, hid it behind her desk.

The children begin to giggle, some of them looking at him from behind their hands, others holding their drawings over their faces.

"Jen, I hardly think..."

"Oh, come on. Draw what you know. Draw the Manhattan skyline, show the kids where you work."

Before he could object, she rushed off to the far end of the room to comfort a crying child whose chalk had broken. She had forgotten yesterday was his last day, forgotten he no longer had a place to spend his time.

The children watched him in expectation. He took a piece of paper from the supply table, selected a coffee can filled with broken pieces of pastel crayons. He chose a seat, arranging and rearranging his bulk to fit within the perimeters of the small chair. Ignoring the gaping stare of his tablemate, he told himself he was doing this for Jen. Any moment now, she would surely announce snack time, a bathroom break, or recess, and he would be free to leave, to go on about his day. The boy beside him went back to his drawing. Glancing over the child's small hunched shoulders, Bradford made out a castle. A pink sun emitted yellow rays showing pink on the grey walls.

He stared at his blank paper, thinking of snow, of the mountains of Korea, and of a fear like the one he was feeling today. He'd been too young to go to World War II, so when the Chinese stirred things up in Korea he was glad to go, spoiling for the fight he'd missed. But each day in Songjin he awakened crying, went out and watched boys his own age fall dead. There had been nothing between him and the war except the little he'd experienced of life. Now there was nothing between him and his retirement except all that he had lived through in between.

"You want to try my crayon?" The boy beside him held out a piece of pink chalk. "It makes drawing easy."

Goldie, Jen's retriever, wandered over, settled her greying muzzle on Bradford's knee, her watery gaze questioning his presence. Bradford gave her a reassuring pat, awkwardly closed his fingers around the moist pastel.

Enveloping, encouraging, Jen's voice rose and fell between the unconscious breathing of children, the muted rasping of chalk. Bradford ran the stick of saturated color along the edge of his paper. Watching it soak in, his eyes opened wide, trying to feel the color. Dragging his fingers down the waxy smoothness, he stared transfixed at the elaborate pattern of whorls thrown into relief along his fingertips, at the pastel crayon, settled now in the curve of his fingers. His hand began to move to the imagined pulses of the children.

photo by Katie Utter

photo by Katie Utter

Meditation for Twilight
Albert Huffstickler

Sometimes, far out in space,
I feel my sexuality blossom—
like a hot flash or like
a belated Fourth of July display.
Lights blossom far beyond
my body's reach then
linger on the air
like a remembrance of youth,
of love's first promise
never quite fulfilled, then
fade as slowly as an old man's
hopes—which seem, for better
or worse, to outlive all
the body's capabilities.
And so, I put the coffee pot on
and think of the things remaining
and smoke my pipe and wonder
how I might have delayed
time's reckoning and watch
the smoke plume upward
to my low ceiling, thinking
of all the men who have
thought these thoughts before me

and feel for a moment that
kinship richer than blood,
deeper than time, that thing
that brought us here so
very long ago and caused us
to stay and continue—some
faith we don't even remember
and can never, even now,
really touch.

Washing Helen's Hair
Anne C. Barnhill

Helen kneels on the oak stool in front of the bathroom sink. Her knees, lumpy with arthritis, hit the faded red cushion with a soft thud. Almost dizzy, she rests her head on the cold rim of enamel. With her left hand, she caresses the familiar grain of the wooden legs, feels the varnish and where it has thinned in spots. It is her stool, the one her husband, Alonzo, made for her years ago. She smiles.

"I'm ready, Lon. Waiting." Her voice cracks, not from emotion but from the strain of yelling for him to come to her. He's on the back porch, shucking corn from the garden. He planted only one row this year after she refused to freeze the surplus. She is tired of his garden, tired of the peeling, boiling, cutting, chopping. She needs rest.

"I'm starting without you." She turns on the faucet, letting the water run until it's warm. This resting on her knees isn't as easy as it used to be. But she'd rather feel her feet go numb and walk on prickles than give up her hair day.

She listens for his step, then turns the water on with more force. He'll hear that, certainly. Alonzo could sense waste even with his bad ears. He might pay no attention to her voice, but he'll high-step it into the house to see why she's running so much water.

Sure enough, the slow gallumph of his steady stride up

the hall vibrates the floor. She raises her head and spies him in the mirror, watches as he ambles toward her. His face is tanned from hours spent in the yard, digging roots, poking his fingers in to test the soil. He puts his old felt hat on the hall dresser, then heads to the bathroom. She notices how bent he has become, yet he straightens when he realizes she is watching him. She winces and lowers her eyes. She thinks how his back is now shaped like the sewing needle her daddy used to stitch people and animals back together.

He wears his old white linen jacket, a Sunday morning uniform of years gone by. She used to tease him about looking like the ice cream man, and he'd laugh that gruff chuckle of his, put his arm around her waist, his muscles ropy, like a lasso.

Now his hair, sparse and grey, streaks across his crown in thin pencil lines. Yet he still cuts a fine figure, and her heart beats faster as she watches him, his large, veiny hands hanging at his sides.

"Had to finish the corn. Water hot enough?" Alonzo tests it with his fingers, then bends around her to wash his hands with soap.

"Feels just right." Helen gives him a thorough search, ogling his reflection in the mirror, looking for any corn worms that might have strayed onto him. She does hate a worm.

"Ain't any on me, missy. I got 'em all." He unbuttons her collar, then pulls down the zipper on her dress. She lets the front drop to her waist. He slides the straps of her slip off her shoulders so that he can touch her.

Slowly, he begins to rub the white flesh, kneading gently, ever so gently. Her shoulders, her neck, the back part of her head. He continues to massage the dimpled skin until he hears her "Ah." That's his signal to start taking down her hair from the French twist at the nape of her neck. Carefully, he removes each fancy comb, then gingerly loosens the hairpins.

"I'm tender-headed." She makes a face at him in the mirror. She sees his dark brown eyes crinkle with fond exasperation.

"I know, missy, I know." Her grey curls fall and cover his hands. The strands wind through his fingers. The hair, stiff and wiry, is the color of pewter, and she imagines he's remembering how blond it had been years ago. And how soft.

Helen hands him her brush made of pig bristles. She holds her head straight as he combs through the long rope of her hair.

"Still pretty. Soft like a silk shawl." He bends over, buries his face in her hair, the smell of it sweet and fresh like warm milk in a pail, the kind he used to carry up from the barn when he was a boy. He's told her this before, many times, confessed his love for her smell. He begins to wet her hair, cupping his hands under the faucet, then pouring the warm water onto her scalp.

"Feels so good." Helen leans over the sink, the weight of the water pulling her. Without him to hold her, she thinks she might fall down the drain, like in that silly nursery rhyme: "Oops, there goes Helen down the hole." Alonzo's fingers support her and he begins to make whirls all over her head.

She smells strawberries when he opens the shampoo. Alonzo surprises her with a new brand every so often, and she likes the changes, loves to think of him at the grocery store, pouring over the different bottles, deciding which one she might enjoy.

He begins to hum. A hymn, one of the old ones, "When the Roll Is Called up Yonder." The feel of the suds, the sound of his voice remind Helen of the first time he washed her hair.

She remembers how embarrassed she'd been, a girl barely fifteen and him a man of twenty-three. They'd married in 1935 with little more than a suitcase of clothes to move into the hotel room they'd let from old Mrs. Abernathy. Helen laughed.

"What's so funny, missy?" He still scrubbed her head, cleaned it good, the way she liked.

"Oh, nothing. I was remembering how scared I was of you back when we were first married." She placed her hands on her thighs and pinched to get some feeling there. Not ready for him to stop, she hoped to delay the inevitable numbness.

"Scared of me?"

"Yep. Especially on our wedding night. And when you wanted to bathe me and wash my hair, I didn't know what to do. It's kinda funny now." Helen grinned. Thinking back took her mind off the pain creeping into her legs.

She could see him as he was then, a tall, gangly man with dark curly hair and a black mustache. She'd been in the bathroom, sitting on the edge of the claw foot tub, her fingers poised above her head, ready to take down her hair. She'd felt his strong hands on hers as she reached for the combs.

"Let me help you." He removed them, then ran his hands through her hair, his thick fingers easing out the snarls.

"Be careful, Lon. My scalp is real tender." She felt the familiar bunching of her muscles, her whole body tense against his touch.

"I won't hurt you." She realized she stood before him in the light, wearing only her undergarments. A hot blush began on her chest.

"I'll bring in a chair. You'll strain your back leaning across the tub like that. We'll wash your hair in the sink, then I'll run your bath water." He raised her up, brushed the hair away from her eyes. While he went to get the chair, she wanted to slip into her robe, the one she'd embroidered for their honeymoon. But she just stood, her bare feet against the cool linoleum floor.

"This'll be a lot easier. Sit down and lean over the sink. That's it." With her back to him, she felt her neck bend, thin as a bird's. Her head heavy, she felt him take the weight of her skull in his hands. He stroked her crown first, then began to wet her hair.

"Your hair's the first thing I noticed about you. Yellow, shimmering in the sunlight." Lon had never been a sweet-talker, hadn't ventured much conversation in his lovemaking. But now, his voice was soft, easy. She relaxed into it. He began to hum that Steven Foster ditty about the girl with brown hair, one he used to sing under his breath when they'd courted in her parent's front parlor.

Soon, her head full of bubbles, Alonzo raised her to a sitting position and piled her hair in a variety of shapes on top of her head. They laughed at the "hairdos," a long spike, a blob with a curl at the tip. Later, clean from her bath, her hair slightly damp, he'd taken her to their bed.

The sound of his voice snaps her back into the real world, the world where her knees ache and her legs, no longer smooth and pearly, are speckled with blue splotches. The world where her golden hair is now the dull color of storm clouds.

"Tired?" He's already rinsed her hair and now holds a large yellow towel slung across his forearm. Yellow's her favorite color, and he always uses the big fluffy one he gave her several years ago.

"My legs are as numb as rubber and my feet have gone plumb to sleep."

"We'll manage, missy." He smiles at her in the mirror.

Helen catches his hands as he starts to wrap her head in the towel. They are rough hands, familiar. Age spots, brown and ragged, ride the veins. These are hands she can trust, hands she has trusted for most of her life. Helen notices a trembling in him. He is tired, too. She brings the callused fingers to her mouth and kisses them, her dry lips leaving a hint of moisture.

"Thank you." She whispers the words, not certain he can hear her.

He gives no reply, just pats her shoulder and leads her to the overstuffed chair on the back porch where he will towel-dry her hair, the drying faster there in the sun.

Helen allows herself to be led, her hand in his. She sinks back into the chair. He lifts her feet, one at a time, onto the hassock, then rubs them for a moment until they are buzzing with warmth. Then he begins to comb her hair carefully, so as not to pull a single strand.

The Fallout Fantasy
John Laue

(After reading Joseph Campbell)

The kids think I'm an old man
in his dotage,
and I'm old all right
compared to them
and even most of their parents;
but I'm not really old
as old goes.
And I won't give up teaching yet.
At least another year,
I've said for a few years now.
And the years build up
like mountains I climb
growing higher and steeper.
I've made a tentative wish
for the very last one
to be a volcano.
When I reach the top
I'll dive into its crater
and shoot out. Yes!
My spirit will float
light as thin ash
all over this marvelous world.
It'll coat the eyelids of fine women,
get in their husbands' armpits,

sift throughout the toes of children,
lodge in the navels of those people
whom I'm curious about,
be eaten and passed
by animals, fish, and birds,
penetrate hell again and heaven
and all places in between.
And when it's traveled enough,
been part of many lives and deaths,
it'll gather, coalescing
into a me without ego, fear, or fantasy.
Then I'll be a new man!

Laundry
Grace Butcher

At the home of the man whose wife has died
laundry flaps on the line,
lively and colorful.

He has it all figured out now,
the moves one makes
to make things clean and usable.

The blue work shirts, the flowered sheets,
the green and white towels
billow in the warm wind,
collecting something of the sun
for him to fold away later,
filling the closet with fading light.

Everything is pretty much the same
though only half of what it used to be.

No dresses brush against the shirts.
The towels will wear out soon,
and then those young colors will be gone
and he will buy maroon and brown.

He doesn't think about it, he simply tromps
down into the dimness of the basement

she used to call "the dungeon" with a laugh,
pulls the pile of damp clothes out
and carries them up out of darkness toward the sun.

And suddenly he stands as if struck
by the thought of her emerging from this dark:
year after year her body rising toward the sky,
the basket of clothes that had been renewed,
to be hung like prayer flags, offerings of love,
to a god who should have responded.

And now all he, the man, can do
is stand at the top of the steps
between the basement and the yard,
the basket in his hands, half blinded by the sun,
the light surging around him as tangible as water.

This is where she stood each week,
rising from the dark below as if
from a grave, over and over again,
never thinking about not being able to do it
one more time. He squints against the sun,
hangs the clothes. The sheets take the wind,
their faded flowers suddenly so bright
they hurt his eyes.

photo by Roger Pfingston

The Chance of Snow
Kathryn Etters Lovatt

Dawson gave Russell Owings his blue speckled cup with the rooster on it. He kept the yellow one, a mama hen with three biddies, for himself. Neither man offered his hand. Dawson, a farmer his life through, grain and vegetable to start with, all timber in the end, had gotten enough hand-shaking these last couple of days. It had not once come natural to him. For a young man like Russell, who routed wood and mixed stain, Dawson guessed it was about the same. His palms were probably as thick as hide.

"You needn't have come out," Owings apologized. Etta's old hound pawed the fencing like he was ready to climb over. Nothing Dawson did kept him down.

The young man squatted into a bare patch alongside the pen and rubbed behind the dog's ears. "My wife sends regards. Too cold, you know, to bring the baby out."

Dawson nodded in agreement. A brood of sparrows huddled at one end of the power line, not a twitter between them. "I do believe we're in for it," he said.

Russell blew at the rim of his cup, and a breath of coffee with real cream and half a spoon's worth of sugar wrenched a warm, sweet hole in the air. "Sure feels like it."

"We got a fire made."

The Dawson house, set this summer for a coat of paint, looked as sad as the afternoon. Smoke barely topped its chimney before being swept up by the day's weather. "You're welcome to come on inside and get warm." Dawson stopped short of offering food. Etta always fixed a ham to take to the grieving family, a fresh ham and a big dish of candied potatoes. Dawson's mouth flooded with the memory.

He could picture his wife as she moved about, sink to stove, making everything by idea and pinches. Inside the lap of her flowered apron, she would wipe her hands of cloves and sorghum, grated orange rind. Dawson imagined butter melting between her fingers, new crop pecans on her breath. He saw her lift the roaster out of the oven, the steadiness of her strength surprising him. It never ceased to surprise him.

How Dawson longed to bring this beanstalk of a boy into that very dream, Etta in her kitchen, let her fatten him up.

"I'm not dressed to visit," said Russell. "I just walked over to see how you were fixed for the night. I could wrap your pipes."

"Not but one outside," said Dawson. "I got it cut off." He studied Russell, who looked shy of twenty, though Dawson knew he was way past. He couldn't judge anymore; everyone looked young to him. "You're fine," he told Russell.

Russell always looked fine. Etta used to say what a wonder he was. "A cabinetmaker," she mused, "and him so neat and clean all the time. Not afraid of his height either." The last jab went to Dawson, who argued he couldn't help his slouch, that his spine had buckled from stooping over fields all these years.

Dawson studied Russell. No trace of gall about his face, there was no spite in the boy's eyes. He tucked his shirts inside his pants, wore lace-up boots. He didn't seem to care about a watch. Dawson so strongly approved of all he saw that he forgave Russell his twenty-odd acres. He repented every oath he'd sworn when Russell bought it out from under his nose. Paid asking price. Asking price. Ah, he was just a kid. A kid who wanted to be out of town a little ways and saw his chance. Dawson felt he knew something about that now, felt he knew all manner of things about his neighbor.

After a day's work, for instance, right before supper, Dawson would bet a sou the boy rolled his sleeves beyond his elbows, that he lathered his arms and scrubbed with a vengeance about his neck. Dawson figured this out the other night when he stood helplessly in back of Russell. He watched the boy's head bend to Etta's, his mouth covering every trace of hers, watched as he wrestled her poor bosoms like yeast dough. He blew into her, blew, blew, blew. Blew, even though, maybe, Etta was already gone.

Russell's neck didn't have a lick of dirt around it, Dawson took note of that fact. What's more, his red flannel shirt held dampness at the wrists, and his collar lay soaking wet all around. He wore an undershirt with a clipped label. Factory second. Dawson had a few himself. Funny, thought Dawson, what you see when you can't think. Funny, how you remember a body's shoulders free of sun, a button hanging on a thread.

"It might be snow to start with," predicted Dawson. "Sooner or later, it'll turn to ice."

The cold went through his one suit, wool, chaffing him

in the stride. It settled on his head, and he wished for a hat. When he was as young as this fellow here, he had a fine crop of hair himself, browner though, much browner than Russell's, and wavy. It began to grow thin about the time he turned sixty, thin but silky, and white as a petticoat. "Etta was scared to death of ice," he said. "Afraid she'd fall and break her hip and never be right again."

When Russell rose up, the dog gave a long, plaintive whine and laid his head on the rim of his food dish. He had a bowl of scraps he wouldn't touch. "Damn dog," thought Dawson, because he was used to saying it to Etta.

"Damn dog," he'd say when it would rain and she would bring him in. He stunk up the house like a barrel of wet burlap.

"Lewis Dawson," Etta would click, "you know good and well you love that old mutt."

"An animal can tell when things aren't right," Russell said. An orange streak of dry pine needles caught in the cuff of his jeans; he picked them off a couple at a time. "He's trying to put it together."

"I reckon you heard him the night through," said Dawson. "He's got a howl to wake the dead." Dawson's heart clenched. Oh, hell. He could feel it coming, another swell of despair working its way to the surface. He put his cup on the gate post and took out his handkerchief. He wiped his eyes clean. Old men's tears, he noticed, came thick with matter.

Russell kept his own eyes low. He pressed his lips together so hard they turned white.

"I don't think it's even hit me yet, not truly. Me here

alone. Etta down there."

"I can understand how you feel," allowed Russell. "Somebody sweeping the yard one morning, gone the next. I can hardly believe it myself."

"She's not buried half a day," Dawson drew in a last mild sniffle, "and here comes the devil." The two of them crooked their heads sideways to see up between the tree branches, loblolly pine and bare oak.

"Heavenly days," said Dawson. Russell and the dog both came to attention. "A saying of Etta's," he remembered. "She'd forget the iron. Or leave her peas boiling. She'd see how late in the day it was getting and what she still had to do. 'Heavenly days,' she'd say. The same thing in the same voice every single time. And then, all in a bustle, she'd have to run off and mind things."

The entire sky looked like one huge field of wet cement this afternoon. No place to fall but down, and by the time it hit ground, the ice would be merciless, and every bit as hard as mortar. That little tent the funeral home had left over Etta's grave would be no match for sleet. The canopy would fall under the thrash of the storm, fall on the flowers and on Etta. And he, too, would be cold tonight. The extra blankets, wherever they were, would drown him in camphor. They would weigh him down without warming him through.

Dawson felt his grief lift a little when he considered all this. A certain vexation even came over him. He felt irritated at Etta herself, leaving so abruptly. On the brink of the weekend, to boot, so the service fell on a Saturday.

Worse, on this particular Saturday, a winter storm overhead.

She died in the evening, which counted. They calculated those few hours into a whole day, and so the first day was lost. Friday, the second day, had been one question after another. Caskets, flowers, what would she wear? Who would carry her? And there was the obituary, all that straining to remember who Etta's original people were and who might be left among them.

Every waking minute till today, until the service itself, he had something else to think about. And now, the chance of snow. This mix of circumstances, Dawson realized, undermined proper mourning. They took away from Etta's dying.

People's minds were on slick roads and the supermarket. They looked ahead toward hazard, then on to thaw, and further still, to where the world fell back to normal. Dawson knew there was no chance of that for him. Nothing would ever be the same.

"Etta," he thought, "how could you?"

Under Thursday's perfect skies, she had hung two loads of wash on the line. Dawson had watched from the backdoor window. It was so bright out, everything acted like a mirror. Even Etta's sheets, fresh out of Clorox, glared. Her duster had never been so yellow.

"Take advantage of this," she had warned her husband. "Get up and do what you can, while you can."

Maybe she had done too much.

She never could sit still. She wouldn't listen either.

"Things can sure change in a hurry," he told Russell, who shook his head in melancholy agreement. Dawson realized he'd been accorded his first genuine silence since Etta had fallen out at the supper table.

"She never did say she felt bad," he confided finally, softly. He fingered two pennies in his pocket, a black walnut.

"Maybe she never did feel bad, Mr. Dawson. Maybe she never knew what hit her."

It would have been a good thing to hear if Dawson hadn't known better. He kicked a pine cone, a hard green one. He felt it on all his toes. As much as he gave for these dress shoes, and no more leather than that.

"She knew," he said. Pain had knocked the breath clean out of her. She had looked across to Dawson with such surprise, her hand not to her heart, but at the hot blade of her shoulder. He saw the pain all right, saw that she understood the truth of pain like that, what it meant, and he saw that she did not fight against it. "I wish I'd been up the road checking the saplings," Dawson confessed. "I'd rather have found her already gone."

"I don't guess you ever get over it," Russell said.

"You go on," said Dawson, who had a war behind him.

"I don't see how."

It came to Dawson all of a sudden how bad it had been on the boy, him seeing the meanness of death, kissing it. Seeing Etta's death at that. She had helped rock the colic out of their newborn.

"You want to go first if you can," Dawson warned him. "It's better all the way around."

Dawson opened the gate and slapped his hand on his

knee for the dog to come on. Both of them needed to get out, go walk, if not up to the mailbox or over toward the creek, then just stretch their legs around the yard. Russell fell in line next to Dawson; the dog wedged himself in the middle.

"Had it been the other way around, Etta, she would be inside that house there. She'd be holding up everybody else," said Dawson. Russell admitted it was probably so. "Me, I'm a worry to them. No one knows their duty. Who's to stop me now, they wonder—I wonder it myself—from doing as I please?"

Russell stopped and checked one of the red shutters. It hung a little off. "Just what is it you want to do?" he asked.

"Son," Dawson said, "you haven't been married long enough."

The dog went straight for the front porch and sprawled across the welcome mat. His jowls flapped over his huge front paws. He looked a sight, sick to the heart.

"It's nothing I want to do exactly, it's what I get a mind to do. Wild hairs." Dawson could tell he wasn't getting through yet. "Say there comes a pile of snow tonight."

"There's a snow," said Russell. "All right."

"And tomorrow, I think I'll dig out."

"Go on."

"Why, Etta, she would call me a fool to my face, an old fool. She'd say, 'You'll drop dead, Lewis Dawson. Mark my words, you will drop dead, and I'll die trying to drag you in.' I would get the shovel out of the barn anyhow. Maybe I'd get outside and go to work. Etta would fret at the door. She'd see my mistake and walk out a little piece—no sign of a sweater or nothing over her shoulders—she'd stand there with her arms wrapped in front of her, shivering, and she'd holler out, 'Stop, Lewis. Please stop! You are giving me the sick headache.'"

"And?"

"And then I could cuss and throw down my shovel, and I could come inside the house."

"Ah," said Russell. He had to laugh. Dawson too.

"Men don't have half the good sense a woman does," Dawson admitted. He hoped Etta felt satisfied somewhere, hearing him say it.

Neither man's coat was enough with this wind, whipping as it did right into the porch well where they stood. The window panes to the living room trembled trying to hold against gusts that backed up and divided and slid in through the cracks anyway.

Some of the children, not Dawson's grandchildren, who had brains to know better, but children of cousins and children of people who called themselves cousins, were sitting in those funeral parlor chairs right before the windows. So was Willis, Dawson's brother. A half-brother he was, from their father's second wife. Stiff as a brush, his shrunken hands propped on his Masonic belt buckle, he had fallen into a wide-mouthed sleep. Willis was living proof of where loneliness could drive a man.

Dawson could see all his company from here, the only thing out of eye's view was the right arm of the kitchen and the two dim bedrooms behind the hall.

"Not much of a house," said Dawson.

"It's a good house," said Russell and petted the boards under his hand. He moved by the window and looked in as well. "I've always liked this house."

"Not much to keep up. A little dark maybe, but easy on Etta's eyes. They were giving her a fit."

"Too late a frost this winter." Russell wiped the glass. "Hard on anybody allergic."

"They were old, that's what she said." Now Dawson wondered what it really meant, why her whites began to burn, why her irises turned so tearful a grey they were practically see-through. "She should have seen about them."

"More food." Russell pointed to the pasteboard bucket Dawson's oldest girl put on the table. Dawson came close and looked in again.

"They take turns getting after me to eat. All I have a taste for is buttermilk."

Out came coleslaw, rice, and gravy; those wipes for your hands.

"You ever eat any of that chicken?" Dawson asked.

"Once in a while."

"What do you think of it?"

"Beats nothing," said Russell. He smacked his lips.

"Could be," said Dawson, who realized then, that when it came right down to it, a Kentucky fried drumstick might be better than no drumstick at all. "Things sure can change in a hurry."

"You ought to eat," Russell said. "Everybody will stay after you till you do."

"Hmm," said Dawson. "You see anything decent?"

"There's a pie or two. Real tins."

"Widows," said Dawson.

Russell went in closer yet, right at the glass, his breath fogging it. "A cake of some sort. "

"The good ones aren't interested in another husband," said Dawson. "I used to ask Etta, if something was to happen to me, would she marry again."

"What'd she say?" Russell cupped his hands about his eyes and stared hard, but Dawson backed away.

"Oh, you know, different things. 'Lord have mercy, Lewis, you have got hardening of the arteries.' She favored that one. Or she'd say, 'Oh yes-sirree, by all means.' That her next husband was going to be young and rich. A doctor maybe."

"Sounds just like her."

The temperature was dropping fast. Dawson was considering closing the dog in a back room. He'd make a racket, for certain, until he was let in the kitchen. Then he would whine in the kitchen because Etta was gone, and the grandchildren wouldn't be able to stand it and they would cry, "Grandpa, can't we please bring Noodle in front of the fire?" And when they had begged enough to satisfy him and Dawson didn't think he seemed too easy, he would say, "Do what you want. Take him home for all I care."

Maybe then the dog would eat a chicken breast, pulled piece by piece off the bone, offered in a soft little hand. He would have to eat something sooner or later or he'd have to lay down and die.

"Etta wouldn't marry again," he told Russell. "She could have done without me."

If Russell wouldn't come in, Dawson knew it was time for him to go. The air stung to breathe it. Every once in a while, Dawson thought he caught a flake of snow, like a tiny white feather floating from a nest. Everybody would leave soon. They needed to get where they were going before it was too late.

"We're just across the field," Russell said as they came up on the backyard and to the path that would take him home. "You come over any time. You need anything, you pick up the telephone."

There was the moment of parting, which was awkward. It had the two of them bowing and nodding and waving back and forth. Dawson reconsidered the value of shaking hands. If that brief touch could offer some grace around these comings and goings, he was all for it.

That evening, he shook everyone's hand who offered it. He let his daughters kiss him over and over, and he let them fix him a plate of food and put it in the oven.

When they were all gone, even Willis, who would have slept the night through if they had left him be, Dawson remembered Etta. He made himself remember she was not in the next room, but gone for good. What would she would do on a night like this?

She would bathe in the sink, he thought, with a nappy washcloth and Dove soap. She would pull on her gown, still in the drawer, and her robe, on the bathroom hook, and she would borrow some of his long wool socks. She would fill milk jugs with fresh water, just in case, and when she looked outside she would see a fine white veil falling in the porch light. The trees would be leaning forward, every inch of them heavy with ice, and there would be no walkway, only white, the whole world dangerous, but white and brilliant. She would bring in more wood then, and not let the fire go out.

Widow
Eleanor Van Houten

Tomorrow I will take out the dead flowers.
They have faded and withered this long week.
I will wash and return the casseroles
and cake plates to sympathetic friends.
I will go to the market and shop for one.
Tomorrow I will take the dog for a walk
and weed the garden. Tomorrow I will
begin to get my life in order again.

I will not pack away his clothes, just yet.
Standing in his closet I smell his scent,
stroke my cheek with a woolen sleeve,
remembering how it once felt
encircling my shoulders.
On his dresser in a blue Japanese bowl,
a handful of coins from his pocket
and a tangle of old keys.

Choices
Nancy Robertson

He tells her
he cannot take her
home for Christmas dinner.
Too many stairs.
His fingers fuss
with the handles
of the basket
that held the present.

Got to go
busy
lots to do
pats her hand, bye Mom,
leaps from the couch
strides down the corridor
forgets the basket
in his haste
to get away
from this place.

Her chin quivers
face distorts
tears stain
her best dress.

Later
when she sits
at Christmas dinner
with the others left behind
she says,
My son came
to see me today
but I didn't want
to go home with him.
Too many stairs, you know.

Flying Time
Elisavietta Ritchie

"He asked me to fly to Bangkok with him,"
giggles the nurse. I picture my father's
wheelchair sprouting aluminum wings,
his skeletal shoulders growing feathers—
scarlet, vermilion, green—
like a swan sired by a parrot.

"I hope you agreed to fly with him,"
I answer. "He was a famous explorer."
She laughs, slaps her plump palms
against her white uniform.
"Lord, what a spaced-out
i-mag-i-na-tion your daddy's got!"

His blue eyes watch us. I smooth
wisps of hair like down on his skull.
My mad daddy. Here are
the springs of my imagination.
At eighty-four may I too
have license for madness.

Meanwhile, I wheel his chair
to his place at the table
between old Mrs. Silverman
screaming "Sugar! Coffee! More milk—"
and Muggsy sloshing soup on his neighbor.
I set the brakes, fasten his seat belt.

Although my father insists that this trip
he would rather have curry and beer
or smoked eel and vodka,
I spoon pureed liver and unsalted limas
into his mouth quickly before
his fingers explore the plate.

Downstairs, in the Ladies,
by mistake I enter the oversized stall
with handrails, high commode,
the blue-and-white Handicapped sign.
But will there be space enough here
for my wings?

photo by Robert Ullman

Can Opener
Dianna Henning

The cat food is
a small hill in the middle
of nondescript ooze
only the comfortable
dare call gravy.

With palms flat
on his upper legs
the old man bows in
simple thanks. He has
again coaxed open the can,
set the card table;
a Kleenex folded under
the knife and fork.

Tonight it's Friskies Beef
& Liver Dinner,
saltines set to the side,
a mug of warm tap water
to wash it all down.

The man's gaze is tight
to his plate where he carefully cuts
the mound into smaller portions,
prompts with his fork
tidbits of Friskies
onto a cracker he then
mops through the caramel liquid.

Later, his aching hands
find their way into a pan
of the good warm water.
This medicinal soak
tides him over until his next check,
and he's grateful
to have gotten the can open
without help from
the pensioner next door.

The World of Dolores Velásquez
Eliud Martínez

It saddens me not to know what the doctors and nurses talk about when Isabel is not here to tell me in Spanish...*me da mucha pena...me da vergüenza y me da coraje.* More so, it infuriates me that in all my eighty-two years I never learned to read and write, not even in Spanish. What are they saying? *Estas enfermeras y los doctores, ¿qué están diciendo?*

I don't understand these nurses and doctors, or even my own grandchildren. I remember when my sons Antonio and Eduardo used to drop their children off to keep me company, when they were very little, before they started school, and later, after they started going to school, when they were ill and could not go. The children are grown now, but when they were little, I remember that taking care of them used to make me sad, to be sitting in the same room with my own grandchildren, like persons from different countries who are not able to speak the same language. Mexicanos lose the language in this country. I suppose it is bound to happen. Sometimes I would say something to the child in Spanish, to Michelle, for example, and she would blink her eyes and shrug her shoulders, and the same with Eduardo's little boy, or Antonio's girls, though they speak Spanish, but Michelle and her brother would say, "I don't understand what you're saying, *'buela.*" Some of the others, too. Well, at least they knew how to say *grandmother* in Spanish.

The doctor told Isabel that I have to stay here. Isabel, Isabel, I want to leave this hospital. I want to go home, but the doctor told her that I am too ill. He says I need medical attention that I can get only in the hospital. Isabel always wanted us to move in with her, but we were stubborn. She offered many times to take her father and me. When I wanted to move, Antonio did not. "I have too much work, *mujer.*" At his age, nearly ninety years old, and still wanting to work! And the times when he was agreeable about moving, I hesitated, thinking about my mother in her old age. Getting old makes trouble for others, better to stay where we are, I thought. So we never moved in with Isabel and Vicente. Antonio and I could never agree. Is it too late, now? Am I going to get well enough to go home? Isabel is such a good daughter, no one could ask for a better daughter. *Sí, ella tiene razón, pero*...but I still want to go home even though she is right...*pa lo que me queda*... with what life remains to me, why not let me die at home?

I must have dozed off. Isabel is here almost all the time, but when she has to go to the bathroom, or when she goes to the cafeteria for lunch or to the house to sleep, these nurses don't listen to me. To them I am just a dying old woman. They probably think there is nothing more they can do, and they don't speak Spanish either. People in this country should at least know Spanish. There are so many of us who cannot speak English, but for us it is too late to learn. Not for them, they are young, and they should try to learn.

El doctor MacKenzie told me I have to stay here. He is a good young doctor...*es muy bueno*...and he speaks Spanish. *Habla español*...he doesn't need anyone to translate for him. I told him I don't like it in the hospital, and he says, *"Lo siento mucho, señora Velásquez, pero usted está muy enferma."* He and Isabel, I know they are right, but I still wish I could go home.

Here in the hospital it is hard to get a good sleep. Sometimes I get drowsy, and just when I manage to fall asleep a nurse comes and wakes me up to take my pulse or to tell me I have to take a pill. Or a nurse comes in and sticks a needle in my arm while I am sleeping soundly and wakes me up. I look up and there is the white uniform, always one of them here to bother me. Except when I need them. No matter how many times I ring for them, that's when they don't come. I hate it when they don't come to take me to the bathroom and I soil myself. Then they take their time about coming to change my clothes and change the sheets. Is this any way to treat an old woman? Isabel gets angry with them. I don't know what she says, but when Isabel is talking and waving her arms and gets angry, the nurses listen!

Sometimes I wake up during the night and I don't know where I am. Isabel said that she found me in the bathroom the other day, cleaning the bathtub, thinking I was home. I don't remember, but she said so. During the day my sons and their families visit. Usually they take turns and sometimes they come at the same time. With their wives and sons and daughters. At times, the room is filled with visitors. My daughters-in-law, my sons, and my grandchildren, my great grandchildren, but Isabel is always here. Sometimes I don't know who it is that comes up to me and kisses me and says, *"¿Cómo está, 'buela?"* What am I supposed to answer? Depending on my mood, if I feel like making them laugh I will say, *"Bien."* Then I say, *"Bien fregada."* All worn out, ha, ha! Ahh-a-ah! What a wretched life!

They see that I am dying, but they love to make me laugh with their constant joking. Especially my youngest, Eduardo, ¡Que lindo, mi consentido! I used to scold him when he didn't visit me for a long time, always too busy with his work. He's a very important businessman, always dressed up, suit, tie. "I could die here at home," I said to him, "and you wouldn't even know, Eduardo. One day you'll come to visit and you'll find me dead." And in his playful way, he made me laugh, as he always does. "Of course I would know, Mamá, I would read about it in the newspaper." ¡Ah que m'hijo! So silly. Always acting up. Here in the hospital I was remembering the other day, how right after he was born, when the nurse brought him to me to breast-feed, she said, "This little one gave you big trouble, a very difficult time, Mrs. Velásquez." A Mexican nurse translated, *"Este muchacho va a ser muy travieso."* He's going to grow up to be full of mischief. He is my last born. We were very poor in those days. He was going to be the seventh, but I lost the one before him. All of them boys, except Isabel. "No more after this baby," I told Antonio. "We can barely feed the large family we already have."

They grew up so fast. Now I wonder where the years went. How did we get so old? Who would have known that Antonio and I would live so long? Who could have imagined we would have such a large family! Every day they come to visit. Except for Miguel, he is too far away. If only he would write.

"*¡Isabel!* Has Miguel written?"

"No, Mamá, but he telephoned. He's coming to see you, and this time Natalie and Sara and Becky are coming with him. Next week." *Vienen la semana próxima, los cuatro. Los periódicos dicen que viene un norte y que va a hacer mucho frío.* She tells me that the weather reports say a bad norther is bringing some very cold weather when they come.

"This is one of the worst winters in Texas in a long, long time. And you know, Mamá, *Sara habla español*. You'll be able to talk with her in Spanish."

Que bueno, hija.

Last night I was thinking about what it was like to be a girl in the old days. For a long time I could not get to sleep. I was aching all over. *Pobrecita* Isabel. She had fallen asleep in her chair. If sleeping in a bed is uncomfortable, it must be much more uncomfortabe to sleep in a chair. I finally fell asleep. Just before I closed my eyes I was thinking about Miguel's daughters. When the little one was five or six years old, I don't remember exactly, they came to visit. Her sister is a little older, two years, I think. Maybe they were a little older than that, but they were little. One evening the little girls made me laugh so much. I was sitting in my armchair, Miguel and I were watching one of the telenovelas on the Mexican television station. I heard them laughing, and out of the corner of my eye I saw them in the hall. Then I turned my head and saw them. They were laughing, holding hands, going into the bathroom to take a bath, all by themselves, and they didn't have any clothes on. Oh my heavens! *¡Diocito mío!* There they were, little Sara and little Rebecca, just like on the day they were born, and I could not help laughing aloud. Miguel asked me why I laughed. He was sitting on the sofa and could not see his little girls. He asked me again. *"¿Por qué se ríe, Mamá?"* And I told him. "Your little girls, *tus hijitas,* Miguel, they just went into the bathroom. I saw them in the hallway, without any clothes on, just like on the day when they were born, and they were not at all embarrassed about their bodies." Miguel told me that he and Natalie were bringing up their daughters to respect their bodies, to know that there is nothing shameful about the body, and that day, I thought, oh, how different it used to be for girls, for women in the old days! My mother was always telling us girls to keep our knees together, to sit properly. She used to get so angry about the way we would sit. *¡No anden enseñando sus vergüenzas! No se sienten como los hombres.* "Don't sit like the men do. Keep your legs together!"

So I am glad for Isabel, for my daughters-in-law, and for my granddaughters that some things have changed for women. They went to school, they learned how to read and write, and their daughters are in school now. The next generation of women will have good jobs too. My granddaughters take pride in their jobs. Whenever one of them buys a new car she drives it over to show it to me. "Look *'buela,* I bought a new car." *Sí, me da mucho gusto por ellas.* They have good jobs. They buy nice clothing and dress nicely all the time. Yes, they speak English and they drive their own cars and they have their own money to spend. When a woman can drive, she does not have to depend on a man to take her anywhere. Things were much different in the old days. Even so, I always found it very annoying when any of my daughters-in-law or my granddaughters would sit down at the table to eat before the men, or expect to be served, as if they were men. *¡Me daba mucho coraje!* I could not help it. I never could get used to it. How dare they act as if they were men!

"*¡Isabel!* Did you prepare something to eat for your brothers?"

"Mamá, *estamos en el hospital*. We're in the hospital. *Los muchachos* ate before coming to see you."

Wisdom Women
CB Follett

Old women, you were the lattice
for new growing vines, used to tell
how fire was kindled, blazed,
how the years turned and seasons
swelled with new growth.

Dark eyes nearly hidden
you kept the secrets. Waited.
Planned when to fish, plant,
harvest the tall grain. You
instructed girls in the mysteries

of blood and sex,
birth, children. You held the moon
on a silken thread, tugged it
around Earth so cycles interwove

with songs you sang by dark-night
while the moon slept, the sky lit
with thousands of stone fires.
You chanted our histories,
how we moved

across land and streambed to come here,
and when we moved from here, as spring
heated the land, this too would you braid
into the story, spinning it out
in thick plaits.

Now, old women don't tell us
what is carried in their wisdoms.
They live silent,
separate from the rest of us
and the long call of the owl is far.

photo by Barbara Beirne

Prayers for My Aging
Arupa Chiarini

1.
May my body be
an old tree
inscribed by rain,
one rumpled breast
held high
to feel the sun,
one low,
to nurse
the landscape of the earth,
sienna rose of evening time.

2.
May I grow old
with the cypress
by the ocean.
May I be rocked
by the waves,
while my sparse hairs
dance and gossip
with the wind.

3.
May I be the silver birch,
may I stand through the winter,
may I reflect light,
may my desires be written
in black lace calligraphy
on white parchment,
may the universe rejoice
in my beauty.

photo by Teresa Tamura

Romance in the Old Folks' Home

Michael Waters

First he offered to read to her,
but she was afraid
he spoke as Bible-thumper, so declined.

Then he steeped several
herbal teas for her table—
she sipped without looking up.

He scissored photos from weeklies
and taped them to her door,
little windows into the past:

couples skating on Highland Pond,
dancing four days in a marathon,
sleeping on roofs above Flatbush Avenue.

She knew she was being spoken to
in a language long forgotten,
like Latin lost after school.

When she found the horned shell
near her lounge on the lawn,
she pressed it to her ear

to hear the ceaseless *hush,*
knowing longing had replaced
the sluggish creature housed there.

The next evening she appeared
with freshly-washed hair
pinned with an ivory comb,

and brought that shy spirit
her favorite book—
The Marble Faun by Nathaniel Hawthorne

who liked to brood on sin—
while the faint widows flushed
and whispered her name—oh, Anna!—

and she asked him please to begin.

Her Game
Floyd Skloot

The nightly round of gin
rummy and shot of schnapps.
They both play to win.
The TV, one of their props,
flickers unwatched, the tints
wrong, the sound low.

She is eighty-eight. He hints
her mind and wits are slow
now, no match for his. This
is false and he knows it. Another
prop, such banter; it's his
specialty. He calls her "Mother"
when he is close to losing,
Rosie when winning. She'll shake
her head and say, "Choosing
you was a serious mistake."

The time he had fare
left for one only,
she said she did not care
to walk, rode the trolley
home herself, and made
him walk the mile through rain.
She underknocks. Played
perfectly. It's still her game.

photo by Barbara Beirne

Drying Apricots
Maggi Ann Grace

Earlier than light
they coax a stepladder
and pails stained black
to the far corner
of the orchard
where once they wrapped
themselves in blankets
and moonlight, would
have melted into each other
if they could. But now,
branches arc over the ground
that breathes the ripeness
of wounded fruit.
The reach is easy.
It is fruit they have come for,
and they fill their buckets
with echoes of the hollow
sound of flutes,
darkening into fullness.

They carry their harvest,
now heavy between them,
to sawhorse tables.
Their task is familiar
(they have been at it for years):
to discard the stone
that alone seems to couple
this fruit. Wife on one side,
husband, opposite.

Their fingers split the pick
easily without a blade
until their hands web
with juice. And the halves
are arranged to dry
on wooden trays branded
by the process, day after
day after week in a season.
Sun-seared apricots thicken
to a new meat—tougher
than the whole, and sweeter
on the tongue.

Dance
Lynne Burgess

The phone is ringing. The old woman lets it. She sits still in the rocker looking out over the tall August field to the end of the coulee. It is going to be hot again. Hot and humid. Out the south window, Catback Ridge curves still and shimmering green against the pale morning sky. A cloud of dense air rises as the day heats, climbing to blue. The old woman needs to watch it evaporate to nothingness.

She wants to be a plant. A dandelion. So that at the browning end of this life, now that the wind has blown her seed away, she can wilt back into the earth, unnoticed. Not a mother, a grandmother, an old neighbor, a widow. Just a plant. Her bones are light and porous, her short white hair so thin her scalp makes it look pink, her skin dry as summer dust. It is time to loosen her roots from this farm. The old woman sits in the rocker and tries to still everything that moves within her—heart, breath, bowels.

The phone starts ringing again. The old woman gets up and pulls the phone jack out of the wall. She lowers herself stiffly to the kitchen floor and lies spread-eagle, sun warming her, relaxing her. Nan, her oldest, is the hardest to shake free. It is probably her on the phone just now, calling to see about groceries. At least that is the pretense. Really calling to check on her.

Nan doesn't understand. "No, Mother," she always says

when the old woman presses a fifty into her hand. "You need it more than I do." But that isn't the point.

The old woman has systematically given away the contents of her savings account, has emptied her closets, keeping only the most essential cookware, blankets, and furniture. Every time someone stops by, they leave with something. It can be a blue bowl, a red sweater, a pile of embroidered pillowcases, or a worn wing-backed chair. The picture albums have been divided up, old letters tied in bundles according to sender, books offered to the children who have loved them best, mementos given to the grandchildren. The old woman has burned her notebooks filled with years of private thoughts. With each load that leaves the house, by hand, by fire smoke, or by failures of memory, the old woman feels lighter, closer to what she seeks to be.

She keeps only the white cat. And the land. These are two things she doesn't truly own. The cat chose her. And the land, well, the land. She remembers when Henry first brought her to this coulee. She felt like she was absorbing every wren song, every pine scent, every goldenrod, every line of leaf against sky. She hushed Henry's voice and walked into the field where he planned to build their house. Still vivid in her memory are the small yellow butterflies spiraling over spikes of vervain swaying, purple, in the wind. As she breathed, she was soaked by the deep sense that this farm was where she had always been.

The sunlight shifts from east to west, slowly. The old woman feels sweat pool over her upper lip, soak her armpits and crotch. The white cat lies stretched full body along her side. Gravel crunches under tires in the driveway. The old woman's heart speeds up. The cat is instantly on all fours. A car door slams. "Dammit," the old woman mutters. She rolls to her side, then to her hands and knees. Blood pounds in her temples, and she nearly blacks out. The kitchen screen opens. The old woman pulls herself up and sits heavily in the rocker. Nan sets a bag of groceries on the table.

"Your phone isn't working, Mother."

The old woman doesn't answer, just starts rocking.

"Mother, you look flushed. Are you OK?"

The old woman narrows her eyes.

"Mother, please talk to me. Are you OK? I tried to call..." Nan grabs the disconnected phone jack coiling on the wooden floor. She shakes it at her mother. "What if you get sick or hurt? What if something should happen to you?" Her voice is squeaky as if her vocal chords were being squeezed by tongs.

The old woman sighs. They have been over all this before. Something is going to happen, is always going to happen. It is this inevitability that gives her all the courage she needs to live alone, not preserved like a jar of pickles in the safety of her daughter's home. But Nan has always tried to take care of things, control things. When she was a teenager, she nearly killed herself by not eating. The old woman remembers holding Nan's hand across the kitchen table, saying, "Eat this honey cake. It's your favorite." It didn't get better until she stopped thinking it was her job as a mother to make Nan's life right. We are too much alike, the old woman thinks. This daughter wants to intervene in what cannot be stopped. And it feels to the old woman like meddling. So she concentrates on the sound of a morning dove cooing in the pines. The cat settles in for a nap on her lap, sleek and warm.

"All right, don't talk to me." Nan's voice enters her. "A cooked chicken is in the foil bag. I'm putting it in the fridge. If you don't want me to come around tomorrow, you'd better answer your phone." She slams the door harder than is necessary. The white cat looks up, startled.

It has been a long time since Henry died, almost forty years. Some days it seems as if the years they spent together belong to another woman, that when she buried him, her life became something new. On those days, she barely thinks of him. Her memories and dreams arch right over her marriage to her youth. She had lived a restricted city life as an only child in a literary family. She remembers white dresses with eyelets and satin sashes, black hightop boots with pointed toes, afternoons when all would retire to their rooms and read. Most evenings were spent in polite attendance to dinner guests. She had no special friends, even at school. Schoolgirl whisperings and crushes seemed vaguely ridiculous and, more to the point, impossible for her. She lived, solitary, surrounded by adults who liked to argue the fine points of Joyce and Elliot, while sipping sherry.

Henry changed everything. And ever since the white cat squeezed through the backdoor as she was closing it, she has been remembering him. What the cat has to do with him, she doesn't know. How can this slender green-eyed female have anything to do with the big, hard-working farmer who brought her to the coulee and gave her five children? About the only likeness was its mystifying insistence on staying with her even before she began putting out dishes of milk-soaked bread. No matter where she went, outside or in, the cat would find a place to sleep nearby. At night it liked to sleep with one paw on her arm, purring like the distant engine of a mower.

"Henry," she said, years ago, "let's dance." The music on the radio was filling her legs with an unexpected longing to move, to find a way back to the first days of their courtship. She put down the iron and waltzed over to tug the loose straps of her husband's overalls. Henry never danced in public. He even blushed when he had to pass the collection plate at church. He hated standing out in front of anyone. He would move with unusual speed to the men's room if an insistent dowager came after him at a wedding. No, Henry did not like to put his barn of a body on display. The memorable exception was their wedding day. The woman supposed he'd become numb to embarrassment after having stood before the entire town and all her stuffy relatives and said, "I, Henry, take thee, May," so publicly. And then he kissed her. She'd been surprised at the tenderness of his kiss. He was sweating, his face red, his collar looking two sizes too small. But he took her hand, held it in his clammy one and kissed her in front of everybody. And that day he danced, awkwardly at first, but his solid frame found the rhythm of the fiddle. It was as if a spring had welled up through an alfalfa field, irrepressible and pure. And that night, years later, children grown and gone, she remembers that Henry, tired and still sweaty from field work, took her in his arms, and they swayed to the radio music. Until she remembered the hot iron and pulled away to finish pressing out the wrinkles in his Sunday pants.

The cat is warm on the old woman's lap. When had Nan left? It is common for her, these days, to get lost in a daydream. The day is slipping toward evening. The old woman knows that the night sky will be bright with the full moon. She stands, and the cat drops gracefully to its feet, taking the opportunity to clean its forepaw. Yes, she thinks, there will be enough light. She finds her old work boots in the dusty closet and ties them on. The worn leather brings back a memory of haying so strong she can smell the drying windrows. The ridge appears close, possible. Nothing else needed but the starting out.

The trail to the ridge has narrowed to a deer path now that Henry isn't around to keep it mowed. But it is still there. Blackberry canes tear at the old woman's skirt and skin. The fruit's purple juice mingles with blood from the thorns' scratches. It is a soft dusk. The day's heat works its way up through the birch, cooling the woods. A wind blows gnats and mosquitoes away. The white cat has slipped out with her into the evening air. It follows, tail straight up, luminous against the dark underbrush. The old woman has to stop every few yards to let her racing pulse slow. The cat leans against her tired legs, waiting for her to go on. Now she is remembering Nan when she was a toddler. She sees her, blue of eye, silky hair shining like a halo in the sun, squatting by a small grass snake, its head crushed by a car in the driveway. "No no no no no," her daughter was chanting. She watched from the kitchen door. It was Henry who gently lifted the snake, let his daughter stroke the soft brown scales, then threw it into the tangled gooseberries.

A loud whippoorwill startles the old woman. Keep on climbing. Slow and steady. All the time in the world. Her legs are quivering and her shirt sticks to her skin when she finds the place. She rests against a sandstone outcropping until the dizziness passes. Then she turns. Behind her the full moon is rising, vibrating in the sky. Before her the layered ridges deepen into greys as the sun's rose light slips beyond them. Her pumping heart slows. There is a rhythm in the night, of arteries flowing, pulsing crickets, wind rocking trees. The white cat calls to her its lovely query. Down below the old woman can see the farm house, small lodestone beyond whose pull she has climbed. The kitchen light comes on.

"Let's dance, Henry," May says into the night.

Front Porch Partners
Elizabeth Crawford

They suit one another, rocking
together; she in polished oak
spindles, he in overstuffed
maple covered by blue afghan
crocheted in years past.

She hums a song someone
played at their wedding
while he daydreams of dancing
with their prettiest guest.

He reviews images of work,
playing cards, hunting, fishing;
hears creak of wooden oars
cutting through cold morning mist.

She sees an old trundle sewing
machine, the vegetable garden
bordered on all sides by favorite
bright-colored flowers,

photo by Martha Wright

and remembers platters of fresh
fish dragged through flour
then fried to golden crispness
in the hot oil of a black iron skillet.

When a frown strains her forehead,
he pats the back of her hand
which slowly turns upward
palming his fingers, reassuring
that she is still there,
still aware of his presence.

Acknowledgments

Grateful acknowledgment is made to the following publications which first published some of the material in this book:

The Poet from the City of the Angels (Bombshelter Press, 1995) for "Hands" by Michael Andrews; *Corrales Comment,* Vol. XIII, No. 4, April 9, 1994 for "Spring Without Burpee Seeds" by Jean Blackmon Waszak; *Pebbles,* Vol. 1, No. 3, Fall 1994 for "In the Autumn" by William Borden; *For Truly to See Your Face* (Black Hat Press, 1996) for "Dance" by Lynne Burgess; *Karamu,* 1996 for "Nearing Menopause, I Run into Elvis at Shoprite," by Barbara Crooker; *Sou'wester,* Vol. 14, No. 3, Spring/Summer 1987 for "At the Reunion" under the title "Reunion" by Mark DeFoe; *The MacGuffin,* Vol. VIII, No. 1, Spring 1991 for "Manon Reassures Her Lover" by Martha Elizabeth; *Psychopoetica, Remembering and Forgetting,* Spring 1995 (University of Hull, UK) for "Wisdom Women" by CB Follett; *Pinehurst Journal,* September 24, 1993, for "Retired" by Daniel Green; *Plainsong,* Vol. 6, No. 1, Winter 1985 and *Where We've Been* (Britenbush Books, 1989) for "Nothing's Been the Same Since John Wayne Died" by William Greenway; *Willamette Week,* December 17—23, 1992, for "Emmaline" by Willa Holmes; *Coffeehouse Poets Quarterly,* November 1992, for "Meditation for Twilight" by Albert Huffstickler; *If Death Were a Woman,* Spring 1994 for "Instructions for Ashes" by Ellen Kort; *I Know It Isn't Funny But...* (Sunflower Inc. Publishing, 1995) for "Pebbles and Crumbs" by Ric Masten; *St. Petersburg Times,* December 9, 1986, *The Orlando Sentinel*, November 2, 1986, and *The Columbus Dispatch*, March 1987 for "A Woman Like That" by Peter Meinke; *Literally* (Writers' Center of Indianapolis), Fall 1994 and *The Village Sampler,* November 1994 for "Harvest" by Shirley Vogler Meister; *The Work of Our Hands* (The Muses' Company, 1992) and *The New Quarterly,* Vol. XI, No. 4, Winter 1992 for "Spring Cleaning" by Sharon H. Nelson; *With Respect for Distance* (Black Rock Press, 1992) for "For an Anniversary" by Gailmarie Pahmeier; *The Southern Anthology* (Southern Artists Alliance, 1995) for "Queen of Cards and Powders" by William Ratner; *Home Planet News,* Vol. 6, No. 3, Issue #25, 1988, *A Wound-Up Cat and Other Bedtime Stories* (Palmerston Press, Toronto, 1993), *Flying Time: Stories and Half-Stories* (Signal Books, 1992 and 1996 ©Elisavietta Ritchie), and *The Arc of the Storm* (Signal Books, 1996) for "Flying Time" by Elisavietta Ritchie; *Room of One's Own,* December 1995 for "Choices," previously titled "The Mount" by Nancy Robertson; *Prairie Schooner,* Vol. LVIII, No. 3, Fall 1974 for "Her Game" by Floyd Skloot; *Plexus,* Issue #55, May 1995 for "The Man Who Loved the Woman Who Loved Elvis" by Terry Amrhein Tappouni; *Porter Gulch Review,* Spring 1995, for "Widow" by Eleanor Van Houten; *Ms.,* Vol. III, No. 5, March/April 1993 and the *1992 Frederick County Poetry Contest Winners Anthology* for "Reflections in Green Glass" by Davi Walders; *Poetry,* Vol. CXLIX, No. 3, December 1986 and *The Burden Lifters* (Carnegie Mellon University Press, 1989) for "Romance in the Old Folks' Home" by Michael Waters; *Gypsy,* No. 17, 1991, *Mind Matters Review,* Summer 1992, and *The Plaza* (Tokyo, Japan), Issue #25, August 1995 for "The Well" by Christopher Woods.

Contributors

MICHAEL ANDREWS is cofounder/publisher/editor of Bombshelter Press and *ONTHEBUS*. He has published nine poetry books and three poetry-photography portfolios, and he has coauthored a book of poems about Vietnam. He has also finished two novels and a book of philosophy, *The Gnomes of Uncertainty* (Waking World), which is being digitally published on the World Wide Web. He has traveled around the world and is currently living in Los Angeles. *p. 39* §

DORI APPEL is an award-winning poet, playwright, and fiction writer, whose work has appeared in four previous Papier-Mache anthologies. Of her eleven produced plays, *Girl Talk*, coauthored with Carolyn Myers, was published by Samuel French, Inc., in 1992. "Friendship," a monologue from *Female Troubles*, is included in *More Monologues by Women, for Women* (Heinemann, 1996). *p. 61* §

ANNE C. BARNHILL lives in Kernersville, North Carolina, where she writes freelance for area newspapers and magazines. She began writing seriously in 1989, and she won an Emerging Artist Grant in 1991. In 1993 she received a writer's residency from the Syvenna Foundation in Linden, Texas. Her fiction has appeared in several literary anthologies and magazines, and she's been selected as a Blumenthal Writer/Reader for 1996. *p. 173*

BARBARA BEIRNE of Morristown, New Jersey, has exhibited her photography in numerous museums and galleries. She has written and photographed six children's books. She is an adjunct professor at County College of Morris, and is currently pursuing a photography project in Appalachia. The Thanks Be to Grandmother Winifred Foundation has recently awarded her a grant to help fund this project. *p. 215 and 223*

JUDITH BELL lives in Arlington, Virginia, with her husband and son. Her novel, *Real Love*, won the 1989 Washington Prize for Fiction. Her stories have appeared in many journals, including *The Washington Review* and *Snake Nation Review*, and in the anthologies *Farm Wives and Other Iowa Stories* and *A Loving Voice*. An art historian, she writes for *Art and Antiques*, *Elle*, *Omni*, *USAir*, and *The Boston Globe Magazine*, among others. *p. 159*

JEAN BLACKMON is an essayist and short story writer whose work has appeared in publications such as *Puerto del Sol*, the *Dallas Morning News*, and *Tumblewords: Writers Reading the West*. She won a first prize for short fiction from *Writer's Digest*. She lives in Corrales, New Mexico, where she and her husband own a grocery store. *p. 106*

WILLIAM BORDEN's novel, *Superstoe*, was published by Orloff Press in 1996. His short stories have won the PEN Syndicated Fiction Award and have appeared in numerous magazines. He is Chester Fritz Distinguished Professor of English at the University of North Dakota and is Fiction Editor of the *North Dakota Quarterly*. *p. 6* §

LYNNE BURGESS lives in rural Wisconsin. Her writing comes in batches that correspond with time off from teaching adolescents. "Dance" is included in the collection, *For Truly to See Your Face*, due in 1996 from Black Hat Press. *p. 226*

GRACE BUTCHER is Professor Emeritus of English from Kent State University's Geauga Campus. Her most recent book, *Child, House, World,* won the Ohio Poet of the Year award for 1991. She has been competing in track for over forty years. *p. 182* §

ARUPA CHIARINI is Playwright in Residence at Acrosstown Repertory Theater, a grassroots, multicultural theater in Gainesville, Florida. She is proud to be part of the Writers in the Schools program. She has lived in Vermont, Oklahoma, Hawaii, California, and Florida. *p. 216*

PETER COOLEY has published five books of poems, the most recent of which is *The Astonished Hours* (Carnegie Mellon, 1992). He teaches creative writing at Tulane University and lives in New Orleans with his wife and three children. His poem is from a new manuscript to be called *Sacred Conversations. p. 4*

ANN COOPER, a teacher-on-the-trail, has written six natural history books for children, including the 1992 children/young adult Colorado Book Award winner. Her poetry and essays have appeared in the *Christian Science Monitor, Sistersong, Frogpond,* and *Poet Magazine. p. 57*

ELIZABETH CRAWFORD earned her BA in history and English with writing concentration at the University of Wisconsin. She has had poetry published in the *Wisconsin Poet's Calendar* for the past three years and works as the general manager of a bookstore that specializes in gently used, collectable, and new books. She recently began facilitating workshops on Courting Creativity. *p. 233*

BARBARA CROOKER has published over five hundred poems in magazines such as *Yankee, The Christian Science Monitor, Country Journal,* and in over forty anthologies (including four by Papier-Mache) and five books. She has received three Pennsylvania Council on the Arts Fellowships in Literature, raised three children, and is still dancing. *p. 14* §

CORTNEY DAVIS coedited *Between the Heartbeats: Poetry and Prose by Nurses* (University of Iowa Press, 1995) and authored *The Body Flute* (Adastra Press, 1994). Her poetry book, *Details of Flesh,* will be out in spring 1997 (Calyx Books). A recipient of a 1994 NEA poetry fellowship and two Connecticut Commission on the Arts poetry grants (1990 and 1994), she lives in Redding, Connecticut, and works as a nurse practitioner in women's health. *p. 18*

MARK DEFOE is a teacher/administrator at West Virginia Wesleyan College. His two chapbooks are *Bringing Home Breakfast* and *Palmate.* His work has appeared in *Poetry, Paris Review, Sewanee Review, Kenyon Review, Yale Review, North American Review,* and many other publications. *p. 20* §

MARTHA ELIZABETH grew up in Virginia, lived in Texas for ten years, and is now a writer and artist in Missoula, Montana. Her poetry collection, *The Return of Pleasure* (Confluence Press, 1996), won the Montana Arts Council First Book Award. *p. 1*

C.B FOLLETT's poems have appeared in numerous magazines and anthologies, including *Calyx, Slant, The Taos Review,* and *Verve.* She recently won the 1994 New Press Literary Quarterly poetry contest and the 1995 Portland Festival Prize, and she received a Marin Arts

Council poetry grant in 1995. She has published two poetry collections, *The Latitudes of Their Going*, 1993, and *Gathering the Mountains*, 1995. She is also a painter. *p. 213*

MICHAEL S. GLASER is a professor of literature and creative writing at St. Mary's College of Maryland, where he directs the annual literary festival. He edited the anthology, *The Cooke Book: A Seasoning of Poets* (SCOP Publications), and his own poems are gathered in *A Lover's Eye* (The Bunny and Crocodile Press), now in its second printing. He has five children, serves as a Poet-in-the-Schools for the Maryland State Arts Council and lives in St. Mary's City, Maryland, with his wife, Kathleen. *p. 22* §

MARIANNE GONTARZ is passionate about people, particularly the aging process, which she expresses in both her work and her photographs. Her work has illustrated many books, including *Ourselves Growing Older* (Boston Women's Health Collective), *Growing Old Disgracefully* (Hen Co-op), and Caroline Bird's *Lives of Their Own: The Secrets of Salty Old Women*. A transplanted Bostonian, she now happily resides in San Rafael, California. *pp. xviii, 26, and 56* §

KATHERINE GOVIER is an Edmonton native who has lived in Calgary, Washington, D.C., and London, England, and now lives in Toronto with her husband and two children. She has taught at Ryerson and York University in Toronto and at Leeds University in England. She has published three short story collections and four novels. Her recent novel, *Hearts of Flame,* received the 1992 City of Toronto Book Award. Her next novel, *Angel Walk,* is due out in the fall of 1996. *p. 140*

MAGGI ANN GRACE is a poet and fiction writer living in Chapel Hill, North Carolina. She teaches creative writing in the most unlikely settings, but also in schools, summer camps, and through adult education programs. She holds an MFA from the University of North Carolina, Greensboro, and is happy to have her work included in this anthology, her third from Papier-Mache. *p. 224* §

DANIEL GREEN, a social worker for many years, was the executive director of the Red Cross in New York. He started writing poetry at age eighty-two, several years after being widowed. He has since published numerous poems in many journals, and has three collections in print, *Late Start* (1989), *On Second Thought* (1992), and *Better Late* (1995). Now eighty-seven, he is remarried, and he and his wife travel extensively. *p. 152*

WILLIAM GREENWAY is a native of Atlanta and is Distinguished Professor of English at Youngstown State University. He has published five collections of poetry, the latest of which is *How the Dead Bury the Dead*, from the University of Akron Press. *p. 54*

ROSE HAMILTON-GOTTLIEB's recent publications include "Forty Acres" in *Farm Wives and Other Iowa Stories,* plus stories in *Room of One's Own* and *The Elephant Ear.* The theme for *Grow Old Along with Me,* combined with her experience cycling, inspired "Aerodynamic Integrity." *p. 42*

ROBERT L. HARRISON has been published in books such as *At the Crack of the Bat* and

Slam Dunk (Hyperion Books for Children); *Baseball: A Treasury of Art and Literature* (Hugh Lauten Levin Associates, Inc.); *The Best of Spitball* (Doubleday); *Mudville Diaries* (Avon Books); and in *Green Fields and White Lines* (McFarland & Company), his own book of baseball poetry. He now resides in East Meadow, New York, with his wife, Dorothy, and their two sons, Roger and Kevin. *p. 35*

DIANNA HENNING holds an MFA in writing from Vermont College of Norwich University. She was awarded the 1994 fellowship to the Writers' Centre in Ireland, sponsored by Eastern Washington University. She has recently been published in *Sing Heavenly Muse!, Slant, The Lullwater Review,* and *Staple* in England, and her essay on William Butler Yeats was published in the twenty-fifth anniversary issue of *Psychological Perspectives. p. 204*

LOIS TSCHETTER HJELMSTAD is a Colorado piano teacher and author of award-winning *Fine Black Lines: Reflections on Facing Cancer, Fear and Loneliness.* Other work has appeared in various publications, including *The Rocky Mountain News, American Medical News, Health Progress, Your Health, Colorado Woman News,* and *LinkUp* (England). *p. 111*

WILLA HOLMES, a writer, retired high school teacher and, years ago, a reporter/photographer for a weekly newspaper, has four children and ten grandchildren. Her husband, Tom, a retired college counselor, is definitely not the model for Howard in her story. She lives in Troutdale, Oregon. *p. 153*

EUNICE HOLTZ lives on the edge of Cherokee Marsh in Madison, Wisconsin, where she is aware of nature daily. She uses poetry and journaling to hold onto the precious ordinary things of life. "What Do Old Women Talk About" was written in response to the death of a dear friend who chose never to talk about ill health. *p. 136*

ALBERT HUFFSTICKLER, a native Texan, graduated from Southwest Texas State University. Now retired from the University of Texas Library, he is sixty-seven. A Texas Senate Resolution recognized his contribution to Texas poetry in 1989. His last collection, *Working on My Death Chant,* was funded by the Texas Commission on the Arts. *p. 171*

ALLISON JOSEPH is the author of *What Keeps Us Here* (Ampersand Press, 1992). Born in London, raised in Toronto and the Bronx, New York, she currently lives in Carbondale, Illinois. She teaches creative writing at Southern Illinois University at Carbondale. *p. 2* §

PHYLLIS KING has lived many lives in her seventy-five years: college student, mother of four, display manager, librarian (recently retired from New York Public), and finally poet. In the last seven years, she has been published in numerous small magazines. She is married to James L. McPherson. *p. 78*

ELLEN KORT, from Appleton, Wisconsin, received the Pablo Neruda Poetry Prize, authored twelve books, and teaches writing workshops for cancer survivors. Her work has been performed by the New York City Dance Theatre. *p. 122* §

JOHN LAUE, former editor of *Transfer* (San Francisco State University) and associate editor of

San Francisco Review, and also a paranoid schizophrenic, is a widely published prize-winning poet who taught and counseled high school students for twenty years. His poem, "Fallout Fantasy," is from his manuscript, *Wasted Roses,* about his teaching experiences. Now retired, he coordinates readings for his National Writers Union local and is on its steering committee. *p. 180*

KATHRYN ETTERS LOVATT, a South Carolina native, lives and writes in Hong Kong. She has an MA in creative writing from Hollins College, and her stories and poems have appeared in a number of periodicals and anthologies, including *I Am Becoming the Woman I've Wanted* (Papier-Mache Press, 1994). *p. 185* §

ELIUD MARTÍNEZ, novelist, surrealist artist, and amateur photographer, has published a novel, *Voice-Haunted Journey* (1990, Bilingual Press, Tempe, Arizona), the first of a projected trilogy titled, *The Notebooks of Miguel Velásquez.* "The World of Dolores Velásquez" is excerpted from the second novel of the trilogy. A Texas native, he received his PhD in English and comparative literature from Ohio University, Athens. He teaches fiction, film, and creative writing at the University of California, Riverside. *p. 82 and 206*

RIC MASTEN was born in Carmel, California, in 1929. He has toured extensively over the last twenty-six years, reading his poetry in well over four hundred colleges and universities in North America, Canada, and England. He is a well-known conference theme speaker and is a regular on many television and radio talk shows. He lives with his poet-wood carver wife, Billie Barbara, in the Big Sur mountains. He has thirteen books to his credit. *p. 117* §

JAMES LOWELL MCPHERSON, former college teacher, former village postmaster, former Poet Laureate of West Virginia while soldiering overseas in World War II, author of *Goodbye Rosie* (Knopf 1965), has been writing poetry for seventy of his seventy-five years. He is married to Phyllis King. *p. 76*

PETER MEINKE is a poet and short story writer who lives in St. Petersburg, Florida. He read his story, "A Woman Like That," winner of a 1986 PEN Syndicated Fiction Award, at the Library of Congress in December 1988. His book, *The Piano Tuner*, won the 1986 Flannery O'Connor Award for Short Fiction. His latest book is *Scars*, a collection of poems. Retired in 1993, he most recently has been Writer-in-Residence at the University of North Carolina at Greensboro. *p. 83*

SHIRLEY VOGLER MEISTER is an award-winning Indianapolis freelancer with prose and poetry in diverse US and Canadian publications. Her poetry's been in print more than four hundred times, including in Papier-Mache's anthologies, *When I Am an Old Woman I Shall Wear Purple, If I Had My Life to Live Over I Would Pick More Daisies,* and *I Am Becoming the Woman I've Wanted. p. 104* §

SHARON H. NELSON's eighth book of poems, *Family Scandals* (1994), follows *The Work of Our Hands* (1992) and *Grasping Men's Metaphors* (1993) in a series about the constructions of language, sexuality, and gender. She writes essays and political analyses and edits nonfiction in Montreal. *p. 101* §

GAILMARIE PAHMEIER coordinates the creative writing program at the University of Nevada. She is twice the recipient of an Artists Fellowship from the Nevada State Council on the Arts. She is the author of *With Respect for Distance* (Black Rock Press, 1992). *p. 80* §

MARY ELIZABETH PARKER is a poet, essayist, and fiction writer in Browns Summit, North Carolina. She has two published chapbooks of poems, including the prize-winning *Breathing in a Foreign Country*, and has authored several published or soon-to-be-published essays and short stories, including "There's a Place Named France," accepted for broadcast on National Public Radio's *Sound of Writing*. *p. 93*

ROGER PFINGSTON teaches English and photography in Bloomington, Indiana. His poems and photographs have appeared in numerous magazines and anthologies, including *New Letters, Yankee, Artful Dodge, Camera & Darkroom, American Photo, Shots,* and *The Party Train*, a collection of North American prose poems. *pp. 59 and 184*

WILLIAM RATNER lives in Los Angeles with his wife and two daughters, works as a voice-over actor, has published fiction in *Pleiades* and *Taiwan Fiction,* essays in *Coast Magazine* and *TV Marquee,* and reads aloud for a public school literacy program. *p. 62*

ELISAVIETTA RITCHIE's *Flying Time: Stories and Half-Stories* contains four PEN Syndicated Fiction winners. Some of her other books are *Elegy for the Other Woman: New and Selected Terribly Female Poems, Tightening the Circle Over Eel Country* (Great Lakes Colleges Association's 1975—76 New Writer's Award winner), and *Raking the Snow* (Washington Writer's Publishing House 1981—82 winner). She edited *The Dolphin's Arc: Endangered Creatures of the Sea. p. 201* §

NANCY ROBERTSON lives in Prince Rupert, British Columbia. Her writing has appeared in a wide variety of publications including *Room of One's Own, Gallerie: Women's Art, Prairie Fire,* and the anthology, *Gifts of Our Fathers* (The Crossing Press, 1994.) *p. 199*

SAVINA ROXAS, former Clarion State University professor, writes award-winning poetry and fiction, and has recently been published in *Green Fuse, Poets On:, Whole Notes,* and an anthology, *Grandmothers Through the Eyes of Women Writers.* She has a poetry chapbook, *Sacrificial Mix,* and her novel, *A Rocky Shore,* is with Lee Shore Literary Agency. *p. 113* §

SARA SANDERSON is an Indianapolis essayist, book reviewer, lecturer, and poet, having written commissioned lyrics for internationally performed music. A Meredith Fund, Texas, grant enabled her to travel to the Pacific Northwest, now often the setting of her poetry. *p. 121*

DEIDRE SCHERER grew up in New York state in a family of artists. She received her BFA from the Rhode Island School of Design in 1967. A cloth book she made for her three daughters inspired her to substitute cloth for paint, and she has since worked with fabric and thread for more than twenty years. Her images of aging have appeared in more than ninety individual and group shows throughout the United States and internationally. Her work has appeared on the covers of several Papier-Mache books. *cover* §

PAT SCHNEIDER's books include *Long Way Home* (poems); *The Writer As an Artist: A New Approach to Writing Alone and With Others;* and (forthcoming) *Wake Up Laughing.* She is director of Amherst Writers and Artists and AWA Press. *p. 110* §

FLOYD SKLOOT's books include the poetry collection *Music Appreciation* (University of Florida Press, 1994), two novels, and a collection of essays, *The Night Side: Seven Years in the Kingdom of the Sick* (Story Line Press, 1996). He lives in Amity, Oregon. *p. 221* §

TERESA TAMURA, a third generation Japanese-American, is a photographer based in Seattle, Washington. She is an MFA graduate of the University of Washington. Her work has appeared in newspapers, magazines, books, and museums. She was born and raised in Idaho. *pp. 5, 37, 100, 139, and 218* §

TERRY AMRHEIN TAPPOUNI is a poet, novelist, reviewer, essayist, and mother of six. Her chapbook, *Lot's Wife,* from Skin Drum Press, is in its second printing. She is an active member of the Undead Arts Collective, a collaboration of visual artists, writers, and musicians in the Tampa Bay area. *p. 16*

ROBERT DANIEL ULLMAN has been a freelancer working in photojournalism, fine art, and editorial photography since 1974. He has had both one-man and group shows in New York City. His background is in fine art, which is the foundation of his work. Born in New York City, he continues to live in New York. *pp. 25 and 203*

KATIE UTTER lives in Westerly, Rhode Island, and has been taking pictures for most of her life. Two of her photographs appeared in Papier-Mache's *I Am Becoming the Woman I've Wanted.* Being able to capture the spark of a person's true personality in a black-and-white photograph, she believes, is her gift. *pp. 79, 116, 169, and 170* §

AMY UYEMATSU is a sansei poet from Los Angeles. Her first book, *30 Miles from J-Town* (Story Line Press, 1992), won the 1992 Nicholas Roerich Poetry Prize. A second book, *Nights of Fire, Nights of Rain,* is due in 1997. *p. 81* §

ELEANOR VAN HOUTEN is a retired speech therapist who lives on the central California coast with her husband who, despite the content of her poem "Widow," is alive and thriving. Some of her poems have been published in the *Porter Gulch Review. p. 198*

JANE AARON VANDER WAL, born in Hopkinsville, Kentucky, in 1937, lives, paints, and writes on the Bay of Fundy shore, Nova Scotia. She has an MA in painting from the University of California, Berkeley. Her husband is a painter. She has one grown daughter: a jazz pianist. She has been published in *Poetry Canada, Antigonish Review, Fiddlehead,* and other Canadian literary magazines. *p. 60*

LISA VICE's novel, *Reckless Driver* (Dutton 1995), will be issued as a Plume paperback in 1996. She has received a PEN Syndicated Fiction Award and a Ludwig R. Voelstein Foundation Award. She lives in Thermopolis, Wyoming, with the writer Martha Clark Cummings. *p. 124*

DAVI WALDERS is a writer and education consultant. She initiated and works actively with writing groups for battered women and parents of HIV-infected children. Her work has appeared in many publications, including *Ms., Seneca Review,* and *Cross Currents*. Mother of two adult daughters, she and her husband of twenty-nine years also canoe and watch for eagles at their cottage on Maryland's Eastern Shore, where they plan someday to grow old together. *p. 23*

MICHAEL WATERS teaches at Salisbury State University on the Eastern Shore of Maryland. His five books include *Bountiful* (1992), *The Burden Lifters* (1989), and *Anniversary of the Air* (1985), all three from Carnegie Mellon University Press. His awards include a fellowship in creative writing from the National Endowment for the Arts. *p. 219*

SALLY WHITNEY is a writer, mother, wife, and collector of dreams. Her short fiction has appeared in *Catalyst, Common Ground, Buffalo Spree,* and other magazines. She is currently working toward an MA in English with writing concentration at the William Paterson College of New Jersey. *p. 27*

BAYLA WINTERS is a professional portrait photographer, performance poet, media reviewer, columnist, and literary consultant. Widely published, she is a 1996 Pushcart Prize nominee and award winner of the International Women's Writing Guild, New York City. She is the author of five contemporary poetry books; her sixth, *Seeing Eye Wife,* is due out in spring 1996. *p. 38*

CHRISTOPHER WOODS lives in Houston. His plays have been produced in Los Angeles, Houston, and New York City. He has published one novel, *The Dream Patch,* and has completed a new novel, *A Woman on Fire. p. 150*

MARTHA WRIGHT has lived in a small city in the finger lakes area of New York for over thirty years. She brought up three children there and practiced as a psychotherapist for many years. In "retirement" she has turned her attention to photography and poetry. *p. 234*

MARION ZOLA is a screenwriter, book writer, and most recently, a producer. Her first love remains poetry. She worked under the poet John Malcolm Brinnin, and has had her poems published in poetry magazines and several anthologies, including *The Diamond Anthology* and *Poetic Voices of America. p. 82*

§ Denotes contributors whose work has appeared in previous Papier-Mache Press anthologies.

Papier-Mache Press

At Papier-Mache Press, it is our goal to identify and successfully present important social issues through enduring works of beauty, grace, and strength. Through our work we hope to encourage empathy and respect among diverse communities, creating a bridge of understanding between the mainstream audience and those who might not otherwise be heard.

We appreciate you, our customer, and strive to earn your continued support. We also value the role of the bookseller in achieving our goals. We are especially grateful to the many independent booksellers whose presence ensures a continuing diversity of opinion, information, and literature in our communities. We encourage you to support these bookstores with your patronage.

We publish many fine books about women's experiences. We also produce lovely posters and T-shirts that complement our anthologies. Please ask your local bookstore which Papier-Mache items they carry. To receive our complete catalog, send your request to Papier-Mache Press, 135 Aviation Way, #14, Watsonville, CA 95076, or call our toll-free number, 800-927-5913.